HOME
MOUNTAINS

Other books in the Washington State University Press
Northwest Voices Essay Series

Louis J. Masson
Reflections: Essays on Place and Family
(1996)

Stephen J. Lyons
Landscape of the Heart: Writings on Daughters and Journeys
(1996)

Robert Schnelle
Valley Walking: Notes on the Land
(1997)

Sam Wright
Edge of Tomorrow: An Arctic Year
(1998)

John C. Pierce
River Earth: A Personal Map
(1999)

HOME MOUNTAINS

reflections from a western middle age

Susan H. Swetnam

Washington State University Press
Pullman, Washington

Washington State University

Washington State University Press
PO Box 645910
Pullman, Washington 99164-5910
Phone: 800-354-7360
Fax: 509-335-8568
E-mail: wsupress@wsu.edu
Web site: www.wsu.edu/wsupress
© 2000 by the Board of Regents of Washington State University
All rights reserved
First printing 2000

Printed and bound in the United States of America on pH neutral, acid-free paper. Reproduction or transmission of material contained in this publication in excess of that permitted by copyright law is prohibited without permission in writing from the publisher.

Chapter One: "On Entering the Eastern Idaho State Fair" and Chapter Six: "The Pleasures of Solitary Dining" were originally published, in slightly different versions, in *Gourmet* magazine, September 1988 and September 1991, respectively. Chapter Seven: "Looking for Churros" was originally published, in a slightly different version, in the spring 1998 issue of *Rendezvous*. All are reprinted with the permission of the publishers.

Library of Congress Cataloging-in-Publication Data

Swetnam, Susan Hendricks.
    Home mountains : reflections from a Western Middle Age / Susan H. Swetnam.
        p. cm. — (Northwest voices essay series)
    ISBN 0-87422-189-7 (pbk. : alk. paper)
    1. Swetnam, Susan Hendricks. 2. Middle aged women—United States—Biography. 3. Self-realization—United States. 4. Idaho—Biography. I. Title. II. Series.

HQ1059.5 U5.S94 2000
305.244—dc21

00-038175

Contents

Introduction 1

One: On Entering the Eastern Idaho State Fair 7

Two: My National Forest 15

Three: The Worst Christmas 21

Four: The Oldest Questions 33

Five: Elizabeth, the Baby 37

Six: The Pleasures of Solitary Dining 41

Seven: Looking for Churros 49

Eight: Digging Bulbs for the New House 55

Nine: Home Mountains 59

Ten: College Choir 63

Eleven: The Beauty Horse 71

Twelve: Angels at the Door 77

Thirteen: My Father's Work 83

Fourteen: The Firebabe 91

Fifteen: Orion 103

Sixteen: Ordinary Time 107

Seventeen: Sleeping in the Sun 113

About the Author 121

Introduction

WHEN I WAS A TEENAGER and young adult, I did not contemplate middle age. It wasn't so much that I consciously dreaded the thought of being middle-aged, just that, as someone making a life for myself quite different than my parents', I had no idea of what lay ahead, and I was too busy inventing each day and looking to the immediate tomorrow to think about what would come. I hoped vaguely that I would be happy, but I had no images at all, no sense of what it might feel like to be forty or fifty.

I now understand why: I simply was not ready to imagine the complicated kinds of perspective and peace that can come with middle age—couldn't have done so if I tried. For me, middle age has meant realizing that I was finally ready to come home in various ways, and then learning to face the homes that I have chosen. I believe now that I was afraid of peace in my youth, afraid that making choices would trap me. I know now, though, that nothing could be farther from the truth: choices, carefully made, can be the solid bases from which one considers further choices—and one will have to, the middle-aged realize, because life *will* clamor and shift. Middle age isn't about escaping from life, I would tell my younger self at this point; it's about finding the sort of grounding that makes living possible.

The essays in *Home Mountains* are about the ordinary occasions that have led to that kind of grounding in my life, and they cover a variety of subjects. Finding home for me has meant, first, learning to live well in my adopted region, southeast Idaho. It is a place of incredible beauty which I knew was my happy destiny the instant that I first saw it twenty years ago, but a quirky, strange sort of home nonetheless. Finding home has also meant revisiting family romances and events of my young adulthood, and forgiving others and myself. It has meant rethinking my own nature, my own beliefs, then rethinking them again, for middle age teaches that truth must have a conditional edge. It has meant accepting that I have a vocation—teaching—and realizing, somewhat to my surprise, that I am a person of faith. It has meant finally realizing the joy that can come from a long-term love.

Though the essays that follow are about specific moments and topics in my particular life, I hope that readers will find reflections that speak to their own circumstances, and that my reflections will remind readers of the ways that they, too, have found active, thoughtful peace as they have aged. If younger people do read this book, I'd like to think that these essays might give them a more concrete picture of middle age than I was able to manage, and a happier one.

In a way, it's fitting that the essays in this book are about finding perspective and peace, because the literal "home mountains" in my life, the basin and range landscape of the northern Intermountain West, offer those qualities in the most literal ways. The Bannock Range, the Portneuf Range, Oxford Peak, Kinport Peak, Slate Mountain, and all the others that form my daily horizon, are not "pretty" mountains like the Appalachians which I visited in the summers of my youth. On Intermountain West hills, trees lie only in the draws, where creeks run and snow stays late; ridges and summits are bare and windswept. Though many newcomers complain about the nakedness of our mountains, I have always loved their openness. One can see where one is going on them, and every stop brings vistas. The sky is huge, the air expansive enough to clear heads at 7000, 8000, 9000 feet. Our mountains are quiet, except in snowmobile and hunting season.

Most of the year, one can still hike all day and see no one, despite recent efforts by the city parks and recreation department and the forest service to improve trails and parking and to promote visits. Before I saw the Intermountain West, I lived for thirty years without knowing that I was claustrophobic, but the physical relief that washed over me during my first months in southeast Idaho, the bone-deep relaxing that felt new to me, taught me how trammeled I had felt for such a long time. So, for me, "perspective" is fact as well as metaphor, and I think that the spirit of a place which allows solitude and space is present even in the essays which don't directly address landscape.

The essays in this collection were written during a little more than a decade, with the year each was written appearing below its title. Though circumstances have changed somewhat since many of them were written, I have not edited earlier words to conform to current truths, for the individual pieces are meant to chronicle stages of thought and feeling, occasions in an ongoing middle age full of changes as well as moments of stability. Thus, some of the essays which follow stand as snapshots of a past that already exists

only in memory. Most dramatically, the town did find out what happened to Jeralee Underwood a few weeks after "The Oldest Questions" was written: she had been murdered by a serial killer and molester of young girls, a man who now sits in prison. In a gentler key, Elizabeth the Baby is almost a teenager at this writing (early winter, 1999) and acting like one; I did finally see the Mink Creek moose one blizzardy day last February in my national forest; we have climbed Slate Mountain and have lived in the house on Campbell Creek long enough now that some of the bulbs which I transplanted from the old house are wearing out. Some of the essays, in their contrast with one another, chronicle change occurring as this book was being composed, most notably "Orion" and "Sleeping in the Sun."

I'm happy to say, however, that many of the most important circumstances still pertain. I still enter bread every year in the Eastern Idaho State Fair and have always won at least one ribbon; I still run or walk daily in the national forest; Meg the Beauty Horse still expects her carrots and sugar from me; I still go to the Catholic church every Sunday and like ordinary time best of all. Most importantly, perhaps, "married" is still an active verb for Ford and me, and one that defines life.

About a third of these essays were published previously. "On Entering the Eastern Idaho State Fair" and "The Pleasures of Solitary Dining" appeared in *Gourmet* (Sept. 1988 and Sept. 1991, respectively), which has graciously granted permission to reprint them with minor changes. The former also appeared in the magazine *Oh, Idaho* (Autumn 1989) and in the anthology *Where the Morning Light's Still Blue: Personal Essays About Idaho* (Moscow: University of Idaho Press, 1994). "My Father's Work" was first published in *Redneck Review of Literature* (Spring 1989), "Looking for Churros" in *Rendezvous* (Spring 1998). By the time that this book is published, "The Firebabe" will have appeared in *Ring of Fire: Writers of the Greater Yellowstone Region* (Powell,

Wyoming: Rocky Mountain Press), which is in press as of early winter, 1999. All three of these essays appear by permission.

I owe thanks to the editors of all of these publications: William Studebaker and Rick Ardinger, Penelope Reedy, Dante Cantrill, Bill Hoagland, but especially to Gail Zweigenthal, former editor in chief of *Gourmet*, who elected to publish an unknown writer in the pages of that fine magazine. The outpouring of favorable letters provoked by "On Entering the Eastern Idaho State Fair" taught me at the start of my writing career just how magically readers can connect with personal essays, and confirmed my desire to work in this genre.

I owe thanks also to my parents, Jack and Betty Hendricks, who always kept the house full of books and encouraged me to read, and to my students, for I believe that commenting on literally thousands of papers cannot help but sharpen one's own ear as a writer. Most of all, I owe thanks to Ford, to whom this volume is dedicated: the person who makes ordinary time a gentle festival, the person who gave me my own home mountains.

One

ON ENTERING THE EASTERN IDAHO STATE FAIR (1987)

O N LABOR DAY WEEKEND, when my colleagues are doing what normal college English teachers do—grilling, reading, hiking, drinking beer—I live in my kitchen. Forgetting my real life, forgoing my sanity, I concentrate on only one thing: baking bread for the Eastern Idaho State Fair.

I abandon the semester's first round of freshman compositions, any attempt at housekeeping, reading, writing, my friends, my husband, and my cats. It's inevitably the hottest 36 hours of the year. Starting Saturday morning (though judging isn't until Monday morning, entries must be in between noon and 6 p.m. on Sunday), I bake until late, get up at 5 a.m. Sunday, and start baking again. I make an elaborate schedule, figuring out how to time things so that I only need two sets of loaves in my two sets of standard-sized pans at once, how to juggle six recipes that need different rising times and different oven temperatures. I write my timetable on the front sheet of a legal pad (pilfered from my department) and prop it up on the counter. I spill flour. I play Vivaldi and Bach, loudly, and worry about the bread sticking to the towels as it rises. My cats go outside; my husband goes to Buddy's (just what it sounds like). I brush the sweat away and eye the ribbons already hanging on my refrigerator door for reassurance. Though I bake every week, this is the only time that I count ten precise minutes of kneading and use a rolling pin to shape the dough—the way you're supposed to—rather than mashing it down with my hand.

I'm hooked. Two years ago, sentimentally inspired by my remarriage and seduced by the brochure that I picked up (innocent that I was) in a fabric store, I entered a loaf of white bread and a loaf of whole wheat bread in the Fair. I was sure that nothing would come of my efforts, for I'd learned in the five years that I'd lived in eastern Idaho that the state is full of wonderful home bakers—daughters of the pioneers, farmwives who stake their identity, their pride on their work. To make things more difficult, many of them are Mormons, women taught to store mountains of flour and canned goods in their basements, women taught baking as tiny girls at their mothers' sides. What chance did I have, daughter of a woman who relied on Pillsbury and Janet Lee for her bread? Why fool around with that stuff, she had reasoned, as any sensible woman in suburban Philadelphia would have in the 1950s, when they could do it so much better? So, fresh bread was emphatically *not* part of my heritage. When my mother wanted to treat us to "home-made" rolls for dinner, she'd make crescent rolls, the ones that come rolled-up in foil-lined cardboard tubes. To this day, the hollow pop that they make when smashed on the edge of a counter sounds like luxury to me. So, I figured, recreational cook and self-made baker that I was, Easterner that I was, with my adapted recipes from *The Vegetarian Epicure II* and *The New York Times Natural Foods Book*, I'd have no chance actually to win. I had never even *been* to a state fair. Still, it would be fun to enter. I was so sure that nothing would come of my entries that first year, in fact, that I didn't even plan on going up to the Fair to *look* until the next weekend. But, Tuesday night as I scanned the list of results in the paper, there was my name. And I'd won not only a blue ribbon for my white bread, but the $50 special premium that the Bingham County Coop was awarding to the winner in that class.

No matter that some of my colleagues in the department spent the next year calling me "Mrs. White Bread" (to my face).

No matter that the special award that I had won was from a major purveyor of noxious chemicals to the potato-growing world. I was hooked. I entered again the next year—more classes this time—and, though my white bread didn't fare so well, I won a blue for my cracked wheat bread.

This year, the stakes are high. Not only do I want to regain my white bread crown and defend my cracked wheat title; many special premiums are offered, including $50 each for whole wheat bread and potato bread, $50 again for white bread, and three five-pound cans of honey for honey bread. It's going to be a long weekend.

Actually, winning a ribbon in the Eastern Idaho State Fair doesn't quite confer the individuating honors that winning a ribbon in, for instance, the Ohio State Fair does. This says nothing about the quality of the competition—merely that Idaho, because of its size and the natural barriers of its mountains and high deserts, has two state fairs: the Eastern, in Blackfoot (my Fair), and the Western, in Boise. It really ought to have even more. If I lived in the vast western central interior of the state—in New Meadows, say, I'd be damned if I'd drive loaves of bread over a hundred miles one way to the Western Idaho State Fair, much of the trip along the winding Payette River on a two-lane road full of preoccupied Winnebago drivers squeezing one more weekend out of summer and drunk Boiseans cutting firewood. Fifty miles roundtrip from my home in Pocatello to the Eastern Fair in Blackfoot, by comparison, isn't bad, especially given that many of the women against whom I compete come much farther, from places like Rigby and Malad City and Saint Anthony, in pickups full of screaming children. I cruise along in my maverick Nissan, listening to Bonnie Tyler and Joni Mitchell (actually, singing along at the top of my lungs, full of the exhilaration of being *done*), watching the light on the hills, in a very different world from theirs.

After two years, I am still the only person in my circle who enters the Fair. My friends visit the Fair for sane reasons: to eat the wonderful, greasy, curly french fries, or to bet on the quarter horses, or to look at exotic breeds of goats, or to listen, a little bemused, to the Judds. Being an outsider makes entering tricky, though. I *am* convinced that the judging isn't rigged, that the ladies in their ruffled western shirts and pants suits who sit behind the entry table don't cheat and lift up the little fold-over tags with the names on them. The problem is, though, that I have no one to consult, and the Fair's rules seem to change frequently, arbitrarily, and without explicit acknowledgment that things have ever been any different. For instance, this year's booklet casually announces in the small print for "Division II—Baking": "Please do NOT bring baked items on plates, tins, etc. of any kind. Use cardboard covered with foil or clean wrapping paper." In previous years, bulletins have read "Please do not bring *cakes* on plates of any kind" (italics mine)—and all bread bakers have used paper plates.

This makes me very uneasy. Should I take the broadening of the noun to heart and abandon plates this year? If so, how big should the pieces of cardboard be? How heavy?

I learned to pay attention to such things when I entered herbs in the Bannock County Fair as a sort of warm-up before entering the Eastern Idaho State Fair for the first time. On entry day, I clipped big bunches of dill, oregano, mint, and thyme minutes before driving up the bench to the fairgrounds and arranged them proudly in sparkling clean pint Ball jars. They looked so pretty that I nearly tied ribbons around them. But when I entered the barn and set them on the long folding table in front of the heavy-set, tightly-permanented woman taking entries, she looked up at me hostilely. "Where's your plates?" she snapped.

"Plates?" I asked, baffled.

She'd seen fools before. "Says right in the book," she said, thrusting a premium book at me. "Next!" I moved my four lovely jars to a side table, blushing and feeling like I did in junior high school home ec class when I couldn't figure out how to turn on the sewing machine. The next woman in line moved up to the table, and I frantically thumbed through the book. Indeed, I found, after some searching, that the rules *did* say, in small print, "All exhibits will be entered on paper plates"—but that was way back at the very start of the "Agriculture and Horticulture" section, seven divisions, six pages and many classes before "Herbs"— back before the six-row malting barley and the *mangles*, for heaven's sake! Several of the women in line held packages of paper plates, but they were eyeing me suspiciously, with my ridiculous bouquets, and they clearly weren't going to share.

I carried my herbs out to the car, drove down to the 7-Eleven, came back, and stood in line again, my herbs ingloriously lumped on the plates that I'd bought. When I got to the head of the line, I smiled, but the woman didn't smile back—she gave no indication that I'd ever been there before, probably not wanting to remind me of my previous disgrace. I completed the forms and got out of there, fast. Though my herbs did win blue ribbons that year, I've never forgotten the lesson that I learned.

So, if the judges are that picky about herbs, I figure, I'd better mind my P's and Q's for the real competition, the bread, and I'll take both paper plates *and* foil-covered cardboard to Blackfoot this year. Fortunately, the bulletin does spell out in no uncertain terms the requirements for the bread itself: "An excellent loaf of bread should be uniform golden brown in color, oblong in shape, and about 9 x 4 x 4 inches in size. The flavor should be nutty, agreeable to taste, and with no suggestions of sourness. The crumb should be slightly moist, tender, yet not crumbling when compressed, light in weight in proportion to size, even grain. The crust of a standard loaf should be tender and of medium thickness." That's what we're aiming for, the other twenty or so women who enter white bread, the other eight or ten who enter the other classes, and I.

I've been doing my homework over the past year, trying to learn about those other women—not for nothing did I take "Methods of Research" in graduate school. My main source has been the *Blue Ribbon Gazette*, a quarterly newsletter published by a woman from Minnesota and advertised to all state fair entrants in the Baking and Canning Divisions of the Home Arts Department. Though the other subscribers' recipes haven't helped my bread-baking efforts (these women clearly understand that elaborate cakes and pies are the surest way to what most of them refer to as "the coveted purple" [the special sweepstakes ribbon awarded at the judges' discretion to the best item in the whole Baking Division]), I've learned a lot from the *Blue Ribbon Gazette*. For one thing, the women who enter state fairs *are* usually daughters of other women who did; for another, the baking marathons in which *they* engage at fair time shame mine (one quarterly column is called "Confessions of a Blue Ribbon Junkie"). Also, I'm definitely an outsider on a national, as well as a state, level, for most of them are absolute traditionalists about women's roles. Shots of grandchildren dominate the newsletter, usually bearing an editor's comment along the lines of "Isn't he darling?" and correspondents brag of their children's accomplishments. Though I'm sure that the editor is sincere when she asks all members of the *Blue Ribbon Gazette* "Family" to write and tell her about themselves, I'm equally sure that if I wrote to report that I had had an exciting winter—I'd been elected Chair of the State Humanities Council, been appointed Director of Composition at my university, and had papers accepted by *Northwest Folklore* and *Frontiers: A Journal of Women Studies*—my letter would be greeted with polite silence.

These women, too, are fiercely competitive—for those for whom state fairs aren't enough, the publication also announces national cooking contests (the "Kraft Marshmallow Creme 'Easy Secret Ingredient' Recipe Contest," for instance). And they are loyal to their tried and true methods and ingredients. One of my favorite reader inquiries of the last year came from a woman who was upset that Fluffo (a shortening par excellence, apparently) was no longer available in her area. "Would our Family Members be on the lookout for FLUFFO in their area," she asked plaintively, "and would they write Proctor and Gamble requesting their reconsideration if they like FLUFFO? Could we petition the company in some way?"

Finally, I've learned that my competitors are indifferent or oblivious to recent fashions in light, elegant cooking. These women use Crisco, Kraft candy caramels, chocolate syrup, and white sugar with abandon. One recently published recipe for "Mississippi Mud Pie," for instance, calls for, among other things, a container of Cool Whip, a package of Instant Vanilla Pudding mix, and *two* packages of Instant Chocolate Pudding Mix. When anything remotely exotic is used, it is always defined and often misspelled ("Ammaretto [liquer]").

Still, though these recipes will never win prizes for nouvelle cuisine, their creators clearly know what they're doing as far as state fairs are concerned. The most recent issue of the *Blue Ribbon Gazette* includes a blurry polaroid photo of a woman about my age (37) sitting proudly behind a card table covered with row upon row of ribbons arranged in neat overlapping concentric circles, with a big pile of purple sweepstakes ribbons at the top. There must be 300 ribbons on that table. My refrigerator door—with its handful of blues and reds from the County Fair and its two proud State Fair blues above them—looks puny by comparison.

Still, I have more ribbons than the people who call me "Mrs. White Bread"—and I *am* proud of them. As an outsider who has won big prizes, too, I've attracted some attention among the insiders. The first year, when I went up to claim my check, the woman distributing prizes said, "Oh, *you're* the one—we've been wondering."

"My sister wants to meet you," said the woman sitting beside her, checking off names. "Wait a minute." She dashed off. Women started appearing from the shady depths of the barn—but, it turned out, they didn't want really to *meet* me, not what I'd call meeting, anyway—they just wanted to *look* at me, silently. "Hi!" I said, trying to be friendly, to break the awkwardness. "I'm Susan Swetnam."

"Nice to know you," said the oldest one, nodding. They kept looking at me for a few seconds, while I kept smiling resolutely, then they faded back to whatever it was that they'd been doing.

"You're the only non-Mormon to win, ever, I'll bet," my husband (another outsider, another college teacher) suggested later, when I wondered aloud what that had been about. "You're the only name they didn't recognize."

"Still," I said, "it was strange."

"Look at it this way," he said. "Now they *will* know your name."

And it *is* feeling more natural, every year. I've grown to love those few minutes when, cardboard box full of bread in arms, I make my way through the crowds of other exhibitors. They bear armfuls of quilts, wedding dresses, tiny lop-eared rabbits, giant zucchini, awful antique carnival glass, photographs of mountain sunsets, and jars of meticulously packed carrots and beans. Once in the Home Arts Barn, I look surreptitiously at other people's loaves of bread, while they look surreptitiously at mine, and I worry about that little bubble on the top crust of my whole wheat bread. I forget that I have a pile of freshman compositions and a kitchen full of dirty dishes waiting for me. It is the day before Labor Day, I am at the Fair, and I am home.

Two

MY NATIONAL FOREST
(1997)

My national forest is not one of the spectacular ones. It has no geysers, no peaks much over 8,000 feet, no deep canyons or waterfalls or bears. Instead, like so many national forests in the West, it has a name unknown to most outsiders—the Caribou—and it sits in a spot that looks unremarkable on a map, about nine miles southwest of Pocatello, Idaho. The part of the Caribou that I call particularly mine is especially modest: a mile and a half along the north/south tending Mink Creek Road where I run or walk nearly every morning, stretching from the entrance cattleguard to the turnoff road for Scout Mountain.

My national forest does have the Cherry Springs Nature Area, snug down along the creek a few hundred yards west of the road, where cranes sometimes nest in summer, gargling at sunrise as I pass, and to the southeast the head of Scout towers craggy and impressive, a few ridges back. Mostly, though, the setting is what one can see anywhere in the little mountain river bottoms of the Intermountain West. Rounded ridges rise a few hundred feet above the road on the east side, blanketed with sage and juniper and drifts of arrowleaf balsamroot in spring; to the west, beyond the line of red willows that marks the creek, the ridges pop up a little more sharply, a thousand feet or so. In deep summer the stretch can be sere and almost drab, crackling brown vegetation and grasshoppers singing in the heat. In winter, hats of cloud sit on the high ridges one day, then drifts and swirls of snow howl the next, wind easily strong enough to stop a pedestrian.

Though I often remember how lucky I am to have a national forest for my backyard, how exotic all of this is—given my girlhood in the Philadelphia suburbs—long acquaintance has taught me not to romanticize the place. In warm seasons, for instance, it is littered with dead things, testimony to the many cars heading for the greater Caribou beyond—for picnics on Scout or for the two official and many unofficial campgrounds, for the hiking and jeep trails, for the logging operations up high. Some spring mornings, the road is slippery with the greenish-yellow spots of ex-goldfinches. In high summer, snakes of all sizes and descriptions lie squashed where they came to seek road warmth when the draws cooled after sunset. The bodies of feral cats appear, pathetic on the roadside, and every now and then a deer dies in public and sits for months just off the road where it was dragged or crawled, its grin getting ghastlier every day. From repeated experience, I know just how long a skunk carcass takes to decay in various weathers.

My national forest also draws a variety of unglamourous human beings—when the sign says, "Land of Many Uses," it's not kidding. Summer weekends bring campers squatting wherever there's a turn-out, sleeping open or under their trucks. Ominous abandoned cars, plateless, make me cross the road sometimes, though I've never been threatened. Once, coming around a blind corner, I surprised a man peeing next to his dented Buick, in which he had clearly slept. What could we do? We said howdy and waved.

Hunting season is the worst. Technically, one can't hunt in my national forest because of the nature area and the two or three grandfathered inholdings, and most hunters do simply roar through on their way to higher, legal ground—orange-clad blurs in big trucks that almost never move over for runners. Now and then, though, they stop to tear down the "no shooting" signs, and occasionally they put them to more creative uses. One morning, for instance, my husband and I saw a pair of hunters sighting at 6 a.m. from a truck right over one of those signs, down to Cherry Springs.

But hunters are far from the only ones who break the morning solitude. The mountain bikers who come in hordes in summer almost never move their Subaru over, nor do the cross-country skiers. On Memorial Day, Fourth of July, and Labor Day weekends, skinny, glamorous runners appear in force, and they sometimes don't say hello to me—clearly not a real runner with my modest pace and my 47-year-old body. More benignly, neighbors much older than I stroll into the edges of my national forest, setting up Saturday morning routines that last for months. A friend walks her llamas or sometimes, hilariously, tries to run with them. Caravans of Auduboners pass, earnest in their Tilley hats, on their way to Cherry Springs for bird counts. Yellow busses of children come through in May to pass the hours until school is out; white busses of convict laborers come in July to cut brush from around the telephone poles.

In spite of all these human incursions, my national forest is usually quiet early in the mornings, and it insists on its own rhythms. With daily visits over the four years since we moved out from town, I've learned where to look for the surprises that mark the immediate intersections of seasons: to a particular patch of aspens in a north-facing draw for the first fall gold, to Scout itself for the first sugar snow, to the big whale ridge where cornices linger longest in June, to the chokecherry tree that always flowers first. I've also seen the great variety of wild creatures who live along the road—for some species are much better than others at avoiding the cars. Besides the cranes, the Caribou holds geese, and ducks in the little pools where the creek runs close to the road, and mountain bluebirds who prefer one particular tree. It also has eagles. One morning, I watched a young bald fly alone up the creek, so low and smooth that only the sudden hush falling just ahead of him hinted his passing.

Along with the predictable deer and rabbits and assorted voles, my national forest holds some bigger animals, too—though not now and never in history, so far as I can tell, the caribou for whom it was named. There is a moose, who comes down the ridges to the creek. Though I've never seen him, many others have: my husband and several of my friends on their own morning trips to the Caribou, and some drunks fishing out of season who were treed in the dark by the moose several summers ago and had to be rescued by the police, babbling as they climbed down of bear, of sasquatch. My own closest encounters have been with improbable animal jogging companions, notably a skunk who came the other way one day, bounding comfortably along facing traffic like any responsible runner, head bobbing as we passed in a way easy to imagine as a companionable Walt Disney nod. And my bobcat with her little tufted ears, who ran alongside me in a stretch of tall grass once or twice a week all one summer.

In those quiet times, my national forest has given me many gifts. For one thing, it has kept me honest about the discrepancies of head and heart. After the Yellowstone fires, when we lived in town and I knew people working on fire ecology, I used to lecture my Eastern friends when they lamented the ruin of the park. Didn't they know, I argued, that fires were necessary? Didn't they realize what would happen without periodic fires? Did they want the park to be tamed, artificial? But now, as a member of the volunteer fire department that protects my national forest, I keep silent about such things. For I know that, despite the real evidence that fire is sometimes good, if someone set my national forest on fire, after I helped put it out, I would find his house and burn it down.

My national forest also gives me the predictable inspirations born of beta-endorphins and sunrise on ridges. I find help with writing, with problem students from my classes at the university, with friends. I think of good things to do with my Girl Scout troop; I find diplomatic advice to give my teaching assistants.

But the best times that my national forest gives me are the hours when my brain shuts off without my even noticing—when my national forest, like a long-term marriage partner, grants me the substantial gift of not paying attention at every moment. On such days, the rhythms of feet and breath take over, and I run along without a thought in my head, mindless as a hunter, as a moose. On such days, I come home refreshed, and the remainder of the day is touched by the quiet—memories of a pink sunrise glow up in an aspen bowl that I didn't even register at the time, the crackle of the creek running under ice, a flash of magpie crossing the road. And I have noticed the forest giving such charmed moments of mindless solitude to others, too. I've glimpsed prison laborers pausing to look at the sky, schoolkids messing alone in the riffles way down the creek from the shrieking horde, mountain bikers actually stopped for longer than necessary, water bottles long empty, scanning the ridges. I know, too, that up high the good hunters separate and sit for hours, musing as well as stalking.

Such moments, I think, are the strongest argument that, despite all our use, our sullying, these hills and these little mountain river bottoms must be safeguarded. For it is in these very modest "wild" places of the West that most of us, no matter why we thought we were visiting in the first place, remember the pleasure of coming out of ourselves, the joy of being simply eyes and ears and muscle for a while—and the joy of sharing, against great odds of our own making, their everyday peace.

Three

THE WORST CHRISTMAS
(1998)

As winter dawned in 1984, I knew that I was about to have the worst Christmas of my life. I was alone for the first time at age 34, living in a little apartment across the street from the public library in Pocatello, Idaho, three thousand miles from my family in Pennsylvania—not that they could have helped, anyway. My marriage had ended two years before. Though I had been the one to ask for the end and had no doubt that the end was right, I was flattened by guilt. I should have tried harder, I thought; my ex-husband was a nice guy, and the only thing really wrong was that we ended up having almost nothing in common, though we had thought that we did at nineteen. My punishment for hurting him and wanting another kind of life, I believed, would be solitude forever. As an apparent confirmation that promise-breakers like me deserved isolation, the new true love that I had found had decided that he didn't love me—he had told me so kindly but explicitly earlier that autumn, on his way to another woman.

Now, I had no one but a few friends, and I couldn't imagine why they'd want to see me—apt to burst into tears in mid-visit—when they had their own full, happy lives, where others loved them and depended on them. No one needed me, I kept telling myself; no one cared. My very good psychologist tried to help, but within hours of appointments I was back in the fog. On weekdays, I dragged myself to my university teaching job where I distracted myself with students, but on weekends I collapsed. In manic bursts of energy, I would check books out of the library, vowing to fill my time with escape and self-improvement, but the books sat unread beyond the first few pages, and fines grew as I lay on the couch, unable to walk down a flight of stairs and a hundred feet to the book return. My two kittens licked my face all through those twilight weekends, reminding me to feed them and to pretend to feed myself.

The approach of Christmas filled me with particular dread. It had been a holiday of high celebration for my family, a day of great ritual, with invariable Christmas Eve tree trimming and vegetable soup and church; stockings opened in the morning before breakfast, presents after; the same onion dip, turkey, stuffing, and pumpkin pie with the same family talk after grandparents arrived in the early afternoon. For a single woman who had qualified herself for that state, I told myself, there would be no tree, no ornaments, no turkey, no presents from which my grandmother had forgotten to remove the labels ("Susan, horse book"). I taunted myself that I had gotten just what I deserved, for I'd sometimes thought that our Christmases were too predictable—and too full of people. This Christmas day, I knew, would have *no* people, and I wondered how I was going to survive.

Once the day itself was over, I believed that I had a chance. In response to one of my pathetic letters, a friend had asked me to come see her after Christmas in Portland and at the Oregon coast, and I'd booked passage on a train that came through my town at 2 a.m. on December 26. But how was I going to fill the hours until then? One night in the second week of December I remembered a suggestion offered in common by my psychologist and Dear Abby and an overdue self-help book: the alone, the self-pitying, they all said, would feel better on holidays if they did something nice for others. Before the mood could pass, I made myself call my friend Tracy, a single graduate student about my age, to ask if I could cook Christmas dinner for her. "Of course!" she said—for Tracy hated to cook as much as I had loved it before the paralysis began. "Can we ask Carl and Judith too? I think they'll be alone for the holiday, and, if you want to cook here, we can put the boys to bed early and have an adult dinner." "The boys" were the two eighteen-month-olds, Carl and Judith's son Joshua, and Tracy's Bill—the latter the product of a calculated Madonna Mom choice that filled me with awe. I agreed and called Carl and Judith, colleagues also, and they were glad for the invitation.

Within a few days, though, I was amazed that I had been forward enough to horn in on these people's holiday. I called Tracy to offer regrets—but, "You can't, Susan. We're already looking forward to it," she said with conviction that allowed no waffling. "We won't have a Christmas dinner without you—the boys keep us too busy to cook."

The last thing I needed was more guilt, so I pulled my attention back to thinking about the meal. "Cook things you've done before in happy times," said my psychologist. "Remind yourself that there's going to be good continuity in your life—that you're still you." So, I planned the broccoli soup with sherry I'd shared with my ex-husband in graduate school before things came apart; the roast duck which I had made for my true love on an especially romantic night; and the real French bread that Sally, my chairman's wife who had fabulous parties, taught me to make one sunny afternoon in her kitchen. I made myself look at food magazines again, and I added two dishes I'd never made before to the menu: bitter greens salad with pomegranate seeds, and wild rice with sauteed mushrooms. I bought cloth napkins; on one of my manic nights, I stayed up late making napkin rings and a centerpiece.

As Christmas approached, though, no amount of determinedly cheery activity could stem the panic. On the last day of exam week, long after everyone else had rushed home, I lingered in the office, leaving only after the janitor looked in at 4:30 and said, puzzled, "Still grading?" Christmas Eve day—my favorite day of the year as a child—I spent in bed, covers literally pulled over my head, burrowing with the cats and moaning aloud "Alone, alone," until five o'clock. Then I dragged myself to dinner at Sally and her husband's house, a regular Christmas Eve event where I'd gone with both my ex-husband and my true love in years past. This year I was pointedly alone—a pathetic single woman, I told myself. Of course, I became maudlin quickly, despite their real kindness, and, by the time I went to midnight mass, I was a teary embarrassment.

I awoke on Christmas thinking that I had good reason to call dinner in sick and spend the day under those same covers. But I knew that Tracy wouldn't let me, and, with sodden clouds on my heart, I dragged myself into my cold kitchen and started making bread. By four p.m., I was loading the car with boxes of the raw materials for dinner, napkins, and napkin rings—though, in a gesture of sullen rebellion, I left the centerpiece behind. Why pretend that this was festive, I thought, that people were really coming together around this table, that anyone wanted me there?

Though Tracy welcomed me with a hug, I spent the first few minutes in her kitchen fighting the impulse to flee. My blood pulsed with familiar adrenaline panic as I chopped broccoli and trussed duck. The big kitchen in Tracy's upstairs apartment, with its warm afternoon light and high ceilings, had seen *real* family Christmas dinners cooked, I thought—I was out of place here, with my pretentious menu. By the time Carl and Judith arrived, I was weeping silently into the salad greens, though everyone politely ignored my tears. Champagne was opened, and the boys were plopped merrily into the bathtub.

But then, in the silliest, simplest way, everything began to change, as I realized that none of us was going to have a "normal" Christmas. I was reducing mushrooms to crisp brown essences of themselves when I heard a shout of laughter, and the boys burst into the kitchen doorway, making a tottering but thrilling break, escaped pink and fresh from the towels. They giggled at me for a moment, then turned slightly away and saluted the warm kitchen in the most comfortable 18-month old way, arching baby boy streams stretching a remarkable distance to splash on the floor near the far wall. They looked like cherub garden statues, and, suddenly, I found myself laughing aloud. "Bill!" Tracy shouted when she rounded the corner, but Judith, product of an easy-going, large family, sat plop down on the floor laughing before she remembered the requisite "No!" Then even Tracy began to giggle, and the boys got a decidedly mixed message as they were bundled into their pjs.

As I went back to my work, I felt like I'd just visited another world. At my parents', such a moment would have been unthinkable, for no one went naked, ever, at any time, not even at 18 months, and certainly not at Christmas. I couldn't imagine what response anyone would have had to such a display *in the kitchen*—though I knew that it wouldn't have been laughter. But I knew that I loved the reaction I'd just seen, that it seemed very right, and I poured myself a glass of champagne while I added the rice to the mushrooms—a glass for fun now, not like the glasses for forgetting the night before.

Then I added to the confusion myself, for I had no idea about how to extract the pomegranate's seeds for the salad. "I've never even seen a pomegranate before," Tracy said, shaking her head, nor had Carl and Judith. So, I decided that I might as well just slice the thing in half; after all, it was a fruit like a pear or an orange. The skin looked tough, so I whacked it with conviction—and, of course, red juice went everywhere, on my apron, on the table, on the just-mopped floor—. "My God, Susan, you've cut yourself," said Carl, rushing in, and I was laughing so hard that it took me a moment to explain. The panic was gone then, though the cleanup took some time. Once I actually pried the seeds out with a kitchen knife and talked my friends into trying them, though, it became clear that the experiment was a real success... in fact, I saw that there was some danger that no seeds would be left for the salad. So I chased the mothers back to their boys and Carl back to his book. The kitchen began to feel like home, and the smells of duck roasting and broccoli stewing in butter sent the boys to bed.

"Are you at a stopping place, Susan?" Judith asked. "Your dinner looks delicious, and we have some gifts for you to help thank you." Though I protested, I was led into the living room, and we all had more champagne, and, when the packages were opened, I owned a new pale green silk scarf, and a book, and some writing paper, and chocolates from the boys. "This is crazy," I said. But I was hugged and my glass was filled... and then it was time for me to give, for dinner was ready.

I'd never had any of this food for Christmas before, and neither had my friends, but it stopped seeming pretentious after the first bite. First we ate the broccoli soup, richer and sweeter than I'd remembered it, and the bread, which Tracy said was better than Sally's. Then we had the duck and mushroom-studded rice, and good red wine, then salad after, like grown-ups. "I'll never be content with cranberry sauce again," Carl said, on finishing his salad. "These seeds taste so much more interesting, and opening a can is so boring compared to preparing this." Over dinner, my friends began to talk about movies—foreign films that Judith and Carl had seen in New York and Tracy had seen on videotape, popular films I'd seen advertisements for—and they got into wonderful arguments about themes and actors and techniques of shooting. Though I hadn't been to the movies in a few years (for I went to bed at 7 p.m., unless I stayed up all night), I remembered what it felt like to be so interested in something, and remembered films I'd loved as a graduate student in Ann Arbor, where it was impossible to breathe without inhaling movie lore. I mentioned films I'd loved then, the conversation shifted, and it was me who was praising *Truffaut,* and arguing that *Doctor Zhivago* was still one of the finest films ever made. After what seemed like hours, we looked down and noticed that the plates were empty, and we cleared the table.

    Then I realized that I'd forgotten completely about dessert. But Judith had brought the fancy sampler boxes that her mother had sent from Dean and Deluca and Balduccis, and we had more than enough macadamia nut cake, and baklava, rugelach, and panetone. Not once did I think of pumpkin pie. Tracy brought out a bottle of Amaretto, and the talk started up again; I was the one who began the "worst movie ever" competition, and we laughed and laughed as we debated categories. After an hour or two, I rose to go into the kitchen and clean up, but they forbade me ("We'll take care of it in the morning—this was such a treat!"), and we sat and talked long after any Christmas dinner of my life had stretched. Remembering that I had a train to catch to Portland, I switched to the dark, bitter coffee that Judith had brewed, but the others kept pouring themselves after-dinner drinks, talk shifting to students we shared—students who had been irritations a few days before but now seemed winsome and enormously funny. When I left to get organized for the train, they stayed at the table, still in a circle of candlelight. "What a great dinner," they said. "What a treat to share Christmas with you"—and I found myself, for the first time in months, believing that kind words were sincere.

    I learned later that the party had lasted long after I left. Tracy and Judith finished that bottle of Amaretto, and it nearly finished them the next morning when, hung over and sick with its sugar, they stumbled into the kitchen to face the cold, greasy wreck of duck pans. But my life took a quieter turn, and I returned instead to my little apartment, checked my bags, petted my kitties. To keep myself awake for the two hours until it was time to go to the station, I turned on the television. If this had been a night perfect with serendipity, I would certainly have seen *It's A Wonderful Life*—but that wasn't on, nor even *White Christmas* or *The Bells of St. Mary's*. Instead, the only movie running was *Damn Yankees*—certainly apposite in its own way, being one of the worst films ever made. Half-asleep but amused, I watched Lola almost getting what she wanted with Ken doll-handsome Tab Hunter. After a while, I found myself humming along with the silly songs as I watched choruses of professional dancers trying to imagine how baseball players would move. To my surprise, I realized that I was really enjoying myself, was really glad that I could see the end before I had to go because I wanted to be sure to describe this to Tracy and Carl and Judith the next time that we had dinner together.

Then I drove through the empty, echoing streets and the blinking traffic lights to the station. When the train (with its wonderful name, *The Pioneer*) finally rolled up through the haze of snow, three hours late, I stowed my bags and stumbled up to the dark car of sleepers—where I went instantly to sleep myself and awakened only to late sunrise two hundred miles west, rolling through industrial parks and trailer camps west of Boise. I spent the morning reading and dozing and finishing my care package of baklava, managing finally to write a real letter to my mother on my new stationery as I watched the stark Burnt River country of eastern Oregon roll by. I was so content with the quiet that I bristled a little when an old lady came on at La Grande, took the seat next to mine, and tried to draw me out.

At midday, when we crossed the Blue Mountains, I roused myself for a walk and a better look at the scenery. Down on the baggage level, I found what seemed to be the only window on the train that opened and put my head out into air full of falling snow, rich with the scent of wet pine. I stood for a long time, feeling the fresh cut of the wind clear away my train stuffiness. We passed steep banks corniced with drifts of snow, wood smoke rising from isolated houses, pickup trucks waiting for us to clear snowfloored crossings. I lost track of how long I'd been standing at the window until I heard an earnest outburst: "Missy, Missy!" There, from a time machine, was an aging black porter, in train uniform, literally wringing his hands. "Missy, please don't do that," he said. "You could get hurt, and then I'd lose my job." I stared at him, wordless. "A pretty girl like you—what if a branch or something hit you?" he pleaded.

"I'm sorry. I didn't think of that," I said, forcing myself to believe that he existed, and closed the window.

"Thank you, oh, thank you, Missy," he nodded. "That's the way to do it." I went back to my seat and only knew how broadly I was smiling when the old lady asked me what had happened.

Many hours later, at dusk, rolling down the Columbia an hour out of Portland, two men who asked to share my table in the club car bought me bloody marys and asked about my Christmas. When I told them the story, they were vastly amused. "Susan Sarandon should play you in the movie," one said, and I was flattered, though I knew that I looked nothing like her. They complained to me about their Christmases; we had a jolly time for a while, and they invited me to call them in the city for dinner and gave me a phone number.

But I was already getting a little tired of them, so I only said I might, and I went up on the observation level alone to watch the light fade on the river, not very far now to the sea, water beside us already feeling the tides. The velvet cliffs of the gorge flashed by near on the south side, dense with spruce and waterfalls; away in the mist, light echoed from the far Washington bank. I found myself wondering what it would be like to wander in those forests on a winter evening, to clamber up to those half-frozen waterfalls. I vowed to come back another year and explore, to make a reservation for myself at that big inn on the river we'd passed a while back, and I started to scheme about how I was going to wrangle the time off to get away.

Then a family came in, man and woman leaning on each other, tired, kids grasping new stuffed animals. From overhearing their talk, I learned that they were traveling back to the city from Christmas at the husband's parents' house in The Dalles, and, for a moment, I let myself imagine that day—the noise and happy crowding, the familiar routine, the oceans of wrapping paper, the proper Christmas dinner with onion dip and turkey and pumpkin pie, the same Christmas movies on video, the same family stories over dinner—and the loving moments that the couple must have stolen in the midst of all the hours when so many people needed them. Suddenly, the sadness started to well up in me, lead in my stomach, blood racing with the knowledge that I would never have that again—

Then I saw the big kitchen with the little garden cherubs, and felt my new silk scarf around my neck, and remembered the soup and the duck and the exploding, delicious pomegranate seeds, and the merry conversation into the night, and *Damn Yankees,* and the black porter, and the knowledge that I was going to the coast alone and had let strangers buy me drinks but preferred my own company. I started to laugh aloud at the sheer possibility of there being Christmases like this in the world, where you could make things up as you went along, taking whatever crazy gifts the world offered, doing whatever you felt like doing as a character in other people's lives—and in your own. The woman caught my eye and smiled. "You must have had a really good Christmas," she said. For a moment, I didn't know what to say, how to begin to sort out an answer, and I simply smiled back. Then I heard myself reply, "I sure did"—and, to my surprise, I knew that I had just told the truth.

Fourteen years have passed since then. The little boys are big enough now that sometimes when they see me on the street they don't say hello. With undying memories of that clean-up, Tracy has never eaten another duck—but she loves my French bread still. None of us drinks Amaretto. I've learned to cut pomegranates under water, and I've gone walking in those Columbia Gorge woods. And this year, my true love and I celebrated the thirteenth Christmas of our marriage—for, yes, he did have a change of heart, and, no, I wasn't so proud or so taken with being Susan Sarandon that I doubted for a moment where I belonged. Some of our Christmases together have been hard and full of learning, others purely joyful; all have been filled with the assurance of growing, lifelong love. But I know that I will always especially cherish the worst Christmas, a day when friends warmed me and the world showed me how to love surprises again—a day when I hoped merely to survive and found, instead, my own resilience.

Four

THE OLDEST QUESTIONS
(JULY 1, 1993)

I AM DRIVING HOME from work on this sweet July night, the hills impossibly green for this time of year, the air clean and cool, arguing with God. Though I slow for the speed trap as I always do, it's only habit, for I know that the police are much too busy to worry about the odd ten miles an hour tonight.

Instead, they're poking around alleys and knocking on doors on the west side, or out south of the city, helping the 1500 people who have gathered to search for what the newscasters euphemistically call "evidence." Two evenings ago, right about now, Jeralee Underwood, an eleven-year-old girl, was forced into a car by a man she apparently didn't know while she was collecting for her paper route.

This is a very safe place, statistically, and on Sunday mornings, very early when I run, the streets are full of single children nearly lost under their newspaper sacks. No one worries, though about ten years ago three adolescent girls disappeared one summer. One, a babysitter apparently devoid of the suspicious boyfriend that would make all of this a little easier, was found in a wooded canyon by a fisherman a month later. But that sort of thing almost never happens here, and most of our memories are short. So the town shivers tonight, and the hills are full of searchers with walking sticks and sturdy shoes, policemen and firefighters and Boy Scouts and other volunteers, out to find something, anything. We have a large outback here, and only the chance that a kidnapper might be as lazy as anyone else, not inclined to go far from the road, might give them success.

From the school picture that is everywhere today, Jeralee looks coltish, with glasses and bright eyes. She's one of six kids from a working-class Mormon family living in a tract house where the streets are named for contractors' children. She was collecting just inside the downtown, in an area of small houses, some dumpy, some old-lady neat, some with big snarling dogs and motorcycles in the yard. Someone saw her forced into the white (or was it blue?) car by the man in the blue hat around 6 o'clock.

We've been cracking down on crime, such as we knew it, in Pocatello lately. Like so many other places, we've targeted drunk drivers, drug users, and gang members. The newspaper has featured heartrending stories about bereaved mothers and tales of careless recidivism; it has printed photographs of incomprehensible graffiti as proof that California problems have migrated here. Still, we've been winning, we've been assured: every serious candidate for Junior Miss trumpets her SADD participation, the courthouse billboard charts DUI arrests, and the newspaper prints the names, addresses, and sentences behind those statistics; television news stories feature busted methamphetamine labs, paraphernalia seized, juvenile delinquents safely incarcerated.

But this sad litany of irresponsibility, addiction, and petty hormonal malice is very different from the real evil that has suddenly come to town. The stumbling ineptitude of down-on-their-luck poor who blunder drunk into nets specifically set to catch them; the bluster of young men in muffler-less, rusty cars that draw police like magnets, the brawls they have together in back parking lots of discount stores; the homemade cookers in basements guarded by tell-tale rottweilers...with bad luck, this could kill somebody, and sometimes does, but this isn't evil, not tonight.

Real evil is incomprehensible, non-human. What would make someone take Jeralee Underwood? "Bad parts," says my husband, and, of course, he's right. Still, tonight, I find myself back in the oldest questions, the questions that I always thought were tiresome when I was younger. Who knows why evil exists? It just does. But, tonight, under these green hills, that no longer seems enough.

As I make our dinner, I hear the helicopters loaned from the nuclear research complex out on the desert (another arch-evil for some of us here—yesterday), which will cruise low over the hills searching for warm spots. Their humming will carry to town all night long, as they comb back and forth, like the *Rachel* in *Moby Dick*, searching for her lost boat, her lost children in all the vastness of the sea, in a world whose dark, incomprehensible edges we try to ignore by setting up easily managed pasteboard versions of evil and jumping up and down on them. Tonight, though, we cannot ignore that real evil exists, and the world crackles with malice. We cannot manage this, we cannot lecture it and make it go away, because we cannot predict it, cannot know it in the least.

Five

ELIZABETH, THE BABY
(1995)

AT OUR HOUSE, she has always been called "Elizabeth, the baby," to distinguish her from Elizabeth, my grandmother, and Elizabeth, the cat. Of course, she's long past a baby now, gap-toothed at seven, her tumble of baby wisps and curls turned to smooth girl hair, fancy in French braids. I am her proxy Idaho godmother, a role which began on the day when I stood in for her mother's sister away in New York—the day that I looked into the baby's eyes and fell in love. With the other human Elizabeth and my sweetheart, she is one of the few things that ties me to earth when gravity thins.

She is everything that I was not when I was little. Bold, coordinated, aware of her own beauty, she has always known just who she is, where her center lies. When she was a toddler, a clutch of boys—her brother and others three, four, six years older than she—dashed by her at a party, literally spinning her around like a cartoon character and depositing her plop on the floor. I was hurrying toward her when she stood, shook herself, gathered her wits—and dashed after them. The next year, at a steep ski area, when all of the other baby beginners had trundled from the rope tow back to their day care cookies and milk, her teacher took Elizabeth on the chairlift to the adult hill for a spontaneous and free private lesson. "We had a great time!" the instructor said after delivering Elizabeth to her father and me, who had been searching frantically for her. Any day now, Elizabeth will be skiing faster than I do. She already swims better, and she has moved to such a high level in gymnastics that she'll have to commit to competition to advance.

Elizabeth's pets seem to have caught her spirited hardiness. The first, a hamster named Emily, was a career escape artist. Captured several times outside her cage, Emily finally thwarted pursuers to live all one winter in the walls and basement of Elizabeth's house, foraging on condensation and old seminar papers, emerging only in the watches of the night to freeze Elizabeth's insomniac mother in her own wanderings. When the first warm day came, Emily apparently left for the territory, for she was never seen again. Elizabeth's second pet, Buster the budgie, lives on contentedly years after Elizabeth's brother's bird died. Buster himself attempted flight once, but he was less successful than Emily, for Elizabeth's most recent pet, Marie the dog, neatly retrieved him in her soft mouth and deposited him in Elizabeth's lap. Marie, in turn, was blindsided by a car when she was a year old but simply bounced off, none the worse for wear—as Elizabeth herself does when she tumbles on moguls, falls off the balance beam, or crashes the bike on which she has never, ever used training wheels.

Besides her apparently charmed physical life, Elizabeth leads a charmed social life. She draws friends effortlessly, in ways that I, who always had one friend at a time, cannot fathom. People plan birthday parties around her. When her mother was awarded a Fulbright and the family went to France for a year, I feared that Elizabeth would be lonely, but she quickly gathered a little cohort there, girls who cried when she left. When she became six, and I kept a promise by forming a Brownie troop for her, I had to order her to stop mentioning the project after she attracted thirteen eager novices within days.

A second child, she never worries about pleasing people, about being the good little girl that I felt compelled to be, and guilt is not a word that she has ever much used. She says what she thinks, directly—and she lies directly, too. When she was four, she tricked a friend, the achingly trusting Kate, into gushing about how nice Elizabeth's mommy was, then, when the baited reciprocal question came, said with a twinkle, "I hate your mommy." During this period, I sent my grandmother a photograph of Elizabeth in the Easter dress that I made for her, a dark-violet print with a white collar. In this wistful picture, I suggested, she looked like the young Tess of the D'Urbervilles. "She looks," said my grandmother, who has seen a child or two, "like a little dickens."

    She was a fairy child back then. The only sure way to attract her was to ignore her. Wooing her would make her flit away, but talking to the other grownups would always draw her to my lap. She'd even let other children in, like the night she and two friends cuddled in a chair with me at a Christmas carolling party, the night that a familiar Christmas song became forever for us "Reindeer Paws," a title given by Elizabeth, who had interpreted its words in her own way at preschool. In those gentle times, to be near her was to feel her utter, unselfconscious ease. If she was sleepy, she slept, soundly and making contented little snory noises, while the party swirled around her, other children dashing in and out, on a lap, in the grass in the sun, even on the floor by someone she liked—"like a sweet little dog," a friend once said.

    As a young girl, she's lost the most outrageous of the mischief—most of the time—but keeps her common sense. She's a good judge of people, frank about what she herself does well—her math, her reading, her sports—and about what she doesn't, as when she mocks her own out-of-tune voice. She still knows just what to say. A few weeks ago, when the Brownies replied to roll call with their favorite flowers, roses and violets and daisies and other girly things, Elizabeth said, "Pumpkin flowers."

    "Pumpkins don't have flowers!" said Maggie, another child ill-prepared for this—but Elizabeth, of course, was right, and she shifted the moment into her own key, making them all laugh with her, cutting through the saccharine haze.

    She has changed the way that I see the world. When I was an adolescent, I used to wish guiltily that those girls apparently comfortable with themselves, the ones who knew what to say, the ones with the friends, would get a comeuppance sometime, would know what it felt like to be awkward, self-conscious, alone. These days, though, I find myself wishing instead that it's possible for people to know who they are at three, at seven, at sixteen, and still to know at thirty. Thanks to Elizabeth the baby, my envy, my furtive trust in fortune's wheel have gone, and I find myself instead hoping against hope that ease and blithe confidence can last, that happiness is real, that grace can be extended to all of us.

Six

THE PLEASURES OF SOLITARY DINING
(1991)

I AM AMAZED that many people seem to regard solitary meals in restaurants as awkward events, but it is clear that they do. I keep coming across restaurant reviews in which critics praise establishments that provide counters or "singles tables" where people unfortunate enough to be dining alone may share strangers' company in preference to the trauma of a lonely meal. I see articles in magazines for professional women offering hints about how to feel less out of place when making solitary visits to restaurants. Even some of my own closest friends, to my astonishment, assume that dining out alone is undesirable. One, a man who I thought had his priorities in the right place, given the fact that he once backpacked a magnum of champagne into the Wind River Mountains, actually chastised me for eating at Denver's Rattlesnake Club by myself some years ago when that wonderful place was still in business. I should have delayed my meal, he insisted, until he and his wife arrived for the academic conference that we were all attending. "What a shame that you couldn't put it off a night!" he said with pity. "We would have been *glad* to go with you."

    This struck me then, and continues to strike me now, as a silly comment, for dining out alone has been one of my favorite sports ever since I learned to read the street maps of unfamiliar cities. In this particular case, in fact, I had spent much of the afternoon before my trip to the Rattlesnake Club sneaking around the hotel, avoiding anyone whom I remotely knew, to insure that I would *not* have dinner companions. I registered for the conference while a popular early session was in progress, and I made my time in the lobby quick. I did not answer the messages waiting for me when I arrived. I snuck out at 4:30, avoiding even the suburbs of the bar, though my dinner reservation wasn't until 6:30.

I was gloriously rewarded for my insistence on privacy. When I arrived at the Rattlesnake Club, I was seated at a small table with a clear view through the restaurant's high windows and watched a full moon climb over the downtown skyline. In blissful silence, at my own pace and with delightful concentration, I enjoyed a red and golden swirled pepper soup; a salad of arugula, oak leaf lettuce and hazelnuts; a saddle of rabbit with roasted peppers and artichokes; and a flourless chocolate cake with crème fraîche and fresh mint leaves that left me speechless. I also treated myself to the best bourbon Manhattan of my life and to three glasses of varied wines, each of which progressively enhanced my delight in the surroundings. Besides the food and the atmosphere, the evening was memorable for another reason: I spent on one meal the entire three-days' food allowance provided by my university, a theoretically easy feat in most big cities (we're only allowed $20 a day), but one I'd certainly never accomplished before. I left feeling indulged, relaxed, and thoroughly happy, and I think that my presentation the next day was better for my private splurge.

Don't get me wrong; I'm not a hermit. I like the company of dinner companions—the talk and laughter, the little bites of other people's food. I believe absolutely, though, that solitary dining offers a completely distinct and no less pleasurable experience than a convivial meal. I'm not talking, of course, about forced solitude. Eating alone in restaurants *every night* because one has no kitchen and no possible companions and because home is too lonely to endure must be unbearable. What I'm describing is *recreational* dining, voluntary solitude when one is traveling for business or pleasure to distant cities; occasional outings in one's own home town.

Such solo meals allow certain freedoms that no dinner in company can provide. Perhaps the best is the license to concentrate rudely, resolutely on the food itself. Alone, one can focus on how the duck and armagnac pâté tastes with the cucumbers, versus how it tastes with the bread, without the distraction of well-meaning but dumb questions ("Is it good?"). One can slowly taste the wine without feeling pretentious or interrupting conversation. One can, frankly, play with the food, shamelessly eating all of the smoked salmon off of the pasta first, or saving most of it for a last, concentrated bite.

Another pleasure of dining alone is the chance to sample foods and preparations that others may consider strange without having to answer questions or fend off incredulous looks. This has never been a problem for me with my husband Ford (who thinks that it's charming when I down raw oysters with the enthusiasm of a shore bird, though he would never touch one), but it *has* caused difficulties with more casual acquaintances. I'll never forget the night in Washington, D.C., when my stuffed squid in its own ink forced two of my dinner companions to exchange places, with the more squeamish moving out of sight and the braver gazing resolutely at my face, not my plate, throughout the meal. I don't like offending friends and acquaintances, but I also don't like forgoing sweetbreads and nasturtium salad ("How can you eat those *flowers*?").

One pleasure that I experience during solitary restaurant meals—the opportunity to order lavishly without feeling self-conscious—is almost certainly the result of my upbringing, which emphasized sensible frugality. Sad experience has taught me that I am temperamentally unable to order an elaborate, multi-course meal in front of other people. Though one cause of this reticence is certainly logistical (what do cheap friends do while one dispatches soup?), I know that the primary cause is pure, unadulterated guilt. My parents liked food, but they were middle-class careful when dining out, and they expected their children to be the same. I don't think that my mother or father actually would have chided me if I had ordered the most expensive thing on the menu . . . but the air at the table would have changed. Even today, when I have dinner companions, the irrational anticipation of gentle disapproval lingers in my psyche. No matter who my companions are, no matter if I'm paying, no matter what kind of financial windfall I've just had, a personal $60 meal in company is impossible for me. When no one's watching, however, I have no trouble being prodigal—enacting the adolescent rebellion that I never really displayed in the proper season—and it feels *wonderful*.

Besides these culinary and psychological pleasures, dining out alone also paradoxically enhances some kinds of human contact. Serious people-watching becomes possible. At the Rattlesnake Club on that memorable night, for instance, I watched a handsome woman apparently in her sixties sitting with a dazzling, much younger man. They may have been mother and son, but . . . .

I enjoy watching less potentially sensational diners, too: grandparents and grandchildren trying to make contact; groups of women (schoolteachers?) enjoying what is obviously a regular catch-up evening. I have never understood solitary diners who read, for it seems to me that the stories which any self-respecting voyeur can invent transcend any narratives available in restaurant-sized editions.

Conversely, the solitary eater can enjoy the pleasure of being a mysterious stranger to other people. I love controverting people's stereotypes about women dining alone (e.g., they always order the house blush wine; they never eat first courses), and I love overhearing things that conversation would deaden. One night about five years ago, for instance, I was riding Amtrak across the country and stopped overnight in Chicago to go to the Art Museum and the Field, to sleep in a real bed, and, of course, to eat real food. So, I went directly to a steakhouse, where I downed a salad, a huge baked potato, a 32-ounce porterhouse bloody rare, and a liter of red wine. As I finished the latter, I overheard my waiter say to a compatriot in perfect Chicagoese, "These girls, they surprise you sometimes." I take that to be one of the highest compliments that I have ever received.

Perhaps the greatest pleasure of dining out alone, though, is the silence. One can think; one can smile to oneself; one can even compose. Sometimes, meals alone are extremely productive for me—insights scribbled on napkins are as good as any other insights—as long as one remembers to take the napkins. Most of the time, though, solitary meals are simply peaceful interludes, times to escape from the hubbub of a conference or meeting, times to—as my freshman composition students say—just cruise out.

To savor the experience of eating out alone, of course, one must be careful about choosing a restaurant, especially if one is a woman. I have female friends who complain about always getting stuck next to the kitchen when they dine out alone, or being ignored by the servers—but then, it invariably turns out that these terrible things have happened at some chain family restaurant. In my opinion, choosing such a setting for solitary dinners invites trouble. After all, these places tend to employ eighteen-year-old servers, and most people that age have probably never seen a woman doing *anything* alone, much less eating. Adolescent rules apply for them: if a person is doing something solo, the person must have no friends. The solitary female diner, in this mind-set, is clearly some sort of social pariah, and any sane adolescent waitperson will naturally want to have as little as possible to do with her.

I've had the best luck dining alone at places where food is respected, places which have a certain self-assurance, places where customers sometimes even speak foreign languages. Besides the Rattlesnake Club, I've eaten marvelous solitary meals at the

Brown Palace in Denver, at Printers' Row in Chicago (where I was seated in the front window), at Primola in New York City, and at Peter Schott's in Boise. Restaurants that treat single women well don't have to be fancy: I always have fun at the Star Hotel in Elko, Nevada, an old Basque lodging house that provides a complimentary glass of enjoyable plonk with lunch; and at various American Cafes in Washington, D.C., where I eat the three-salad plate and drink imported beer. Despite what some women business travelers' advice manuals say, I've found that the best service comes when I don't dress elaborately; I wear good, tailored pants and a silk shirt, or my plain black cashmere sheath from Royal Silk to the dressier places; nice jeans and a good shirt to the informal ones. Nor do I go through the elaborate reservations rituals that some sources suggest; I would never phone pretending to be my own secretary. I simply make a reservation, appear a little early, request a wine list, and ask informed questions of the waiter or waitress. Looking like one enjoys food, of course, is always helpful.

Being a devotee of solitary meals has compensations that go beyond the single meal. During my first sabbatical, it added adventure to the inevitable stretches of hours before and after libraries and historical societies opened. My project took me around the Northwest—a week in one city, a few days in another town—so I spent a good deal of time alone in new places. How horrible months of room service would have been! Instead, my research trips became culinary vacations. I discovered Olympia oysters in Olympia, the most interesting breakfasts I'd ever eaten at a bistro in Portland, and organic lamb chops in Helena. It was a wonderful semester—and I produced an article and several papers, too, papers which took me to other places where I had other meals . . . .

I've also found that my love of eating out alone enhances romance, for Ford also enjoys solitary restaurant meals. We often separate for lunch when we're in big cities together, to meet in the late afternoon and compare notes over cocktails. The dinners à *deux* that follow inevitably seem like trysts, because we come to them out of choice.

    And so I pity people who don't seem to enjoy eating out alone. It seems crazy to me to prefer the awkwardness of making conversation with lonely strangers at a "singles table" to the experiences which await the solitary diner. Solitary dining is a pleasure, I maintain, vastly more desirable than meals spent in dull company. It offers indulgence; it offers fantasy; it offers simple fun. Most importantly, perhaps, it offers one of the rarest experiences for the busy person, and one of the most precious: the chance to become reacquainted with oneself.

Seven

LOOKING FOR CHURROS
(1998)

ON THIS COOL AUGUST MORNING, Molly Manzanares and I are driving through the rolling sagebrush hills of northern New Mexico, looking for Churro rams. We're jouncing along in Molly's ancient Dodge ram pickup, but the Churros, unable to appreciate the fitness of this coincidence, have so far refused to show themselves. "Last summer they insisted on going in the river," Molly says, guiding the pickup down a rutted two-track between juniper groves toward the Brazos. "They got so filthy. We kept taking them out, and they kept getting back in. The wool washing people complained."

All summer long, I've been worrying about how to talk to the women in Los Ojos, women who began teaching themselves to weave fifteen years ago. Since then, they've built a cooperative business, Tierra Wools, in this remote place, reinventing themselves as supporters of their families—and as artists—as surely as they've reinvented the nearly forgotten Rio Grande weaving tradition. I'm here to do an article for *Handwoven* magazine, inspired by a brief, romantic glimpse of the shady workroom behind their shop. Since the idea was accepted, though, as I've waited for this single free week between my summer semester and fall semester teaching, I've been having serious second thoughts, wondering about my ability to connect with women whose lives are so different from mine.

On the simplest level, I've despaired of literal comprehension. During telephone calls to arrange this visit, I've had to keep asking people to spell things, words which have turned out to be common ones transformed in the pour of northern New Mexican Hispanic English, vowels backed and softened, consonants almost vowels. More seriously, I've been fretting over pace and protocol, worried about my Philadelphia speediness, too quick and borderline rude even for Anglo Idaho, even after twenty years.

"Count to ten before you break in and answer." My husband has spent time in Mexico. "Better yet, count to ten and then count to ten again." He has advised me all through the summer about the ways that one waits, gives space, lets people think. This has helped calm me a little, but I know that I'm still far from prepared. Northern New Mexico has been, after all, contested ground.

"I'd love to move to Rio Arriba County," says a friend who once lived not far from there. "But it would be very, very hard if you were an Anglo. That's where the courthouse takeover was, after all. You'd have to have absolutely excellent Spanish, and even then...."

This morning, though, words are coming easily for Molly and me, as we wander through the meandering paths of the ranch that she and her husband have been running all their married lives. Molly is my age, surprisingly blonde, though she was born here. She helped found Tierra Wools, and she is now general manager, somewhat against her inclination, she confides. She is reticent and soft spoken, thin and tough, and a little weary—the way that a woman with four daughters, a son, and two businesses to mother would have to be in this country. She has a sudden, friendly smile, though, and after two days I am relaxing in her presence. As we drive, she asks me how I come to be a magazine writer as well as a teacher. I find myself talking about the way they align, the delight of guiding beginners in the craft of writing, how proud they are when they first sell a piece. "Like beginning weavers," she nods.

We are on this mission because Molly announced yesterday afternoon that my story needed a photograph of a Churro sheep, the local breed whose wool is used in Los Ojos. It's a good idea, for Churro rams are endearingly photogenic, tough, blocky little animals with curling horns two or three times too large for their bodies. Churros are symbolically important here, for they came north with the first Hispanic settlers from the flocks brought by the Conquistadors, but nearly disappeared, late in the nineteenth century, crossed with sheep which bore finer wool. Today, after careful breeding, full-blooded Churros once again roam these hillsides, bearing drought and cold and rough country. At least in theory they still roam—Molly and I haven't seen a one all morning.

"Maybe they're in the shade in that clump of trees," Molly says. She parks the truck, and we take out on foot, sneaking down to the coolness of the junipers. We walk through bright stands of paintbrush and thistle and lupines, early midsummer flowers where I live, 2500 feet lower. Molly is talking about the youngest of her four daughters, Luisa. The others, stairstepped at fourteen, fifteen, and sixteen, she says, are confident weavers, but Luisa is still finding her way. "I've asked her to put something in the state fair this year," Molly says, "But she's hard to convince." She sighs. "Eleven is such a tough age."

With a flash of joy, I remember that today is my goddaughter Elizabeth's eleventh birthday. I tell Molly this, and immediately we are laughing about the ways of girls, and I am telling her about the scout troop I started five years ago for Elizabeth, and the other thirteen eleven-year-olds I've come to love as a result. Quiet Luisa, whom we left struggling with even tension back in the weaving room, and Elizabeth, my beloved town child with her soccer and her pert confidence, are with us as we search the cool grass under the junipers. I find myself wondering what they might say to each other.

From the moment I arrived, I've realized that Tierra Wools has been presented too simply by the few other writers who have visited. Yes, these women are working class heroines resurrecting their traditional culture and restoring their community's pride—but they are also much more, as complicated and ordinary as the women who will read about them in *Handwoven*. The women in the break room have dignity, but they also gossip and tease. They're not quite uniformly bound in sisterly community, either. One lovely young woman with high Indian cheekbones and another, squat and dark, speak only to each other. "Oh, that's just Maria and Rebeca," the women say, "they keep to themselves." A long-time worker at the cooperative confides that some weavers quit before their work pays but after much effort has been invested in them; others work sporadically, complaining about the expectations. "We have to be good," she says. "But it's so hard for them to see. And they don't want to know what it means to work. I feel sorry for them, but sometimes they make me so angry. I don't know how Molly copes with it."

"Look at that." Molly gestures now across the river to a cluster of new houses on a far hill. "It's hard to believe how much things are changing around here. So many new second homes."

I tell her that this is true in southeast Idaho, too, and I note that the newcomers don't pull their own weight. "I'm a volunteer firefighter," I explain, "and we have two or three big new developments going up in our fire district. Nobody in any of them has offered to join the department—but they gripe about the service."

Molly laughs, shaking her head. "I'm an EMT," she says. "A couple of months ago, we were called to this new gated community. The gate was locked, and it took a long time before we could find anybody who would open it for us. Once we got in there, it was a maze! No street signs, because people don't want other people to know where their houses are! You should have heard them when we finally found the house."

"A gated community?" I'm confused. "What are they gated against, out here?"

Molly's smile becomes a little quieter. "Us, I think," she says.

This is as close as we get to cultural disclosure this morning, and that's fine with both of us. We do talk of things near our hearts—Molly of her father, who is aging and insists on keeping his ranch himself; me of my best friend, now estranged from me because I stupidly offered an unrequested opinion about her fiancé. We also talk of silly things: Molly of a goat, lonely because her kid was taken by a coyote, who lurks by the house looking plaintively in the windows; me about Elizabeth's plaintive postcards from Boston this summer announcing that there is nothing to do in the city. We laugh, and we shrug our shoulders a good deal.

Ultimately, the Churros prove elusive, and we turn back to town, Molly wincing as a beer bottle crunches under the tires as we roll up the ditchbank onto the hard road. She promises to send a Churro photograph. "This was a wonderful morning," she says as we park in the dirt lot across from the weaving shop. "I almost forgot that I had to go back to work."

"Me too," I reply. We grin at each other, conspirators, knowing without saying that we'll both remember this morning—a morning when we, the responsible ones, acted like we had time to burn, a morning when we played frank and delighted hooky, wandering through the hills, imagining each other's lives, looking for Churros.

Eight

DIGGING BULBS FOR THE NEW HOUSE
(1994)

ON THIS WARM LATE OCTOBER AFTERNOON, as I dig bulbs from this big front flower bed, cottonwood leaves drift down from the big junk tree next door, the same one that buries us in a shower of white fluff every spring. Tiny yellow leaves are everywhere, leaves that slip through the tines of rakes and clog the blades of lawnmowers. But this fall, I'm surprised to find myself nostalgic about them instead of shaking my fist at the tree as usual. For this is the last time, the last autumn that those leaves will shower into my yard.

I'm digging one bed every few days now, gathering in all of our hundreds of bulbs as I need to gather in these leaves, from this little house where we've lived all of the eight years since our marriage. This house, impossibly small, dearly loved, with its big west windows, arched inside doorways, and tiny yard, sits just two blocks from the campus where we teach. Finally, at 43 and 52, we're moving to a grown-up house in the hills, a full-professor house taking shape under the bulldozer as I dig these bulbs. There, we'll have things that we need now, things whose absence makes us rub up against each other sometimes, striking sparks, striking fogs of discontent, for all our love, all our trying. In the new house, we'll have two studies, a kitchen where we can both work, a real dining space where our friends can eat without having to worry about knocking the plant shelf onto themselves, a deck, and vistas to clear our heads.

In terms of gardening, we'll have the opposite problem to what we've had in this funny little house. Here, we've had trouble finding room for all the bulbs, all the vegetables, all the herbs, all of the trees and shrubs that we've dreamed of growing. We've shaken our heads sadly for years over catalogue pictures of the fruit trees, banks of fall asters, strange colors of lilacs for which we have no space. Around the new house, we'll have three acres of hillside, plenty of ground to fill in among the junipers. I'll transplant these 300 bulbs, my sorrel and Chinese lanterns and violets, and our lily bed. A friend has agreed to disassemble and move the raised-box vegetable garden that Ford lovingly built with screws against this day—a very good friend, for he has offered to transport also the eight years of compost-enriched dirt that the box contains. We'll take the forsythia and lilac planted just before we were married. Our first anniversary apple tree, though, will have to be left behind, to my sorrow, for it is too big to transplant—time has passed so quickly with us. Still, all the wealth of this narrow yard, where we've made even the sidewalk strip lush with perennial geraniums and thyme and peonies, will look thin out there.

    Digging this biggest bed this afternoon, I'm being careful to go deep, hoping to get all the fancy split-cups and doubles in the daffodil mixture that I planted years ago, especially those funny tiny yellow daffs whose smell overpowers a room. I'm worried, though, that the tiny pips that look like species tulips really belong to the invasive daisy-like flowers that battle with my bulbs in late spring, sending thousands of soft, vaguely chamomile-scented sprouts up to choke the bed in June. I worry that I'm lovingly transplanting my problems up the hill. I'd like to take only the best that we've cultivated here, all the joys of this little house, and leave the incidental trouble behind.

    I do plan to leave some things deliberately—the bed of tulips and crocus that I planted the first year that we were married, the muscari around the tree, the rhubarb, the mint and sage and tarragon and lemon balm. We can always get more of them, and I think that we should have some new plants to toast our new time together. Besides, it seems only fair that this house, which has been so good to us, stays adorned. On this gentle afternoon, thinking about going is easier, indeed, when I know that I'm leaving some tangible memory of our love behind, a surprise of brightness for the next person, the woman who will dig here next October, putting in new bulbs, new hopes of her own.

Nine

HOME MOUNTAINS
(1996)

As it turned out, the steep north slope wasn't terribly icy, and I could pick my way around the rocks, up between the bands of ponderosa pines so prominent from town, all the way to the top. "You're going up there by yourself?" the woman in the next office had asked, looking out my window to Kinport Peak a few hours before. "But it's starting to snow on top." In fact, that was exactly why I was going, on a whim to climb to the first skiff of early November, and to walk up the north face, where I'd never been, with its rubbly little rock bands and clean open lines.

I stood on top in the evening glow, lights just starting to come on in town, looking down the front plunge to the regular trail where I'd descend—no sense getting caught in the dark. But, for a minute, I stood silent, happy with myself for this ad hoc adventure, grateful to know literally another side of the peak that I see every day.

One of the great joys of living in Idaho is the chance for such impromptu adventures on backyard mountains like Kinport, as I discovered when I came to Pocatello in 1979 after graduate school in the Midwest. That first summer, I threw myself into exploring the mountains in my immediate and extended backyard under the guidance of the man who, five years later, became my husband.

In fact, given some of that first summer's experiences, it's a little surprising that we ended up together. One of my first trips was a two-day traverse along the Bonneville Ridge, southeast of

Pocatello—a walk of about fifteen miles which crosses three 8,000-foot summits. Ford, then my husband-to-be, assured me that the walk wasn't technical, and he was right—except that I wasn't really in shape, and my only other mountain experience—along relatively tame sections of the Appalachian Trail—hadn't prepared me for trail-less walking in the July high desert.

I'll never forget how appalled I was when the boulders on the south slope of Mt. Bonneville shifted under my feet as I picked my way through them; or how terrified I was at climbing a steep patch of late snow among the trees; or how much I missed that snow when, later, we ran out of water and I limped out the last two miles, dizzy and sick. Still, I also remember the sunrise on the ridge when we saw the Tetons silhouetted in the rosy dawn, and the bliss of walking down into the cool shade of Harkness Creek at the south end of the ridge and seeing deer. I came to respect backyard mountains on that trip, and I began to love them.

Since then, I've done lots of mountain walking and have learned a good deal: how to ignore my fears and take a short step across a long drop on Mt. Borah; how to manage scree on Oxford Peak; how to scramble down out of a thunderstorm on Tom. I've learned the pleasures of finally getting up a mountain that seemed determined to keep me off: after four unsuccessful tries on the long, dry Oakley side of Cache Peak, we climbed it the honest way, up the steep slopes of the eastern basin above the cirque lakes. Most important, I've learned to drink plenty of water.

And I've learned the delight of getting to know a few backyard mountains thoroughly. In particular, Kinport Peak, on the west bench of Pocatello and the site of my solo "north face" climb, feels like home. After many rambles there, simply glancing from my office window triggers images from many trips. In early spring on a high ridge broken with outcroppings, I've heard the voices of baby coyotes in their dens. In wet Junes, yellow clover reaches waist high, and footsteps release the scent of honey. In fall, the creek bottoms smell darkly of browning scrub oak and aspen leaves and cooling mud. In winter, on the top slopes, junipers ossified with frost lean east, away from the prevailing winds. A certain ridge is where the golden eagles hunt; a particular draw holds a secret forest of Russian olive trees.

 The mountain is also full of the faces of friends. I never go to the summit without thinking of Tracy there, eating the strawberries that I smuggled up to celebrate her one and only mountaineering exploit after months of training; I think of Bill Gibson one Halloween eve, walking out to his truck after going part way up with us, then frightening us in the dark when he came back to greet us on the trail, flashlight under his chin. I remember when Wayne's cheese sandwich emerged frozen solid from his pack one January, when the valley temperature was fifteen degrees below zero, and how we laughed, giddy with the audacity of being on top in that weather. And always, I think of Ford, with whom I've climbed so many times, of his expansive stride along the ridges, his joy in the changes of light, of the things he's written about Kinport. He and I have taken to calling Kinport affectionately "K-1" in honor of its relative importance to us; K-2, in the Karakoram, may be the second highest mountain in the world, but Kinport is the prominent peak in our everyday lives.

 We now have a mountain almost literally in the backyard of our new house south of Pocatello on Campbell Creek. Slate Mountain is modest for Idaho at 7,000 feet, but when we climbed it for the first time, we found it full of surprises. Slate has a long, confused summit ridge with several peaks, abrupt lines of cliffs, and a face broken by rock ribs and steep chutes that hold ice late. We hiked up in April, with spring beauties in the wet patches and snow still high, but I'm eager to see what it looks like now that the sun has baked the ridges clean. I'm also looking forward to the autumn traverses we've imagined, looking down on the dot that is our house as the afternoon darkens. Knowing Ford, sooner or later I expect that we'll be up there in the moonlight.

That's what tends to happen with backyard mountains—once you've climbed a peak a few times, you never see it again in quite the same way. You remember the red and green lichen on the summit rocks, the smell of warm limestone in the sun, the way the light dapples through the aspen along a high creek. You wonder what's blooming now in the meadow where you ate your orange; or, on blizzard nights by the home fire, you imagine what the bursts and drifts of snow look like on the big humpbacked ridge, how cold the wind is up there. It's easy to find yourself obsessed with learning about the peak in all moods, all weathers. Then, someday, you realize that you've lost track of the number of times you've been on top, and you know that the mountain has become your mountain, and you've become its person.

Ten

College Choir
(1997)

One of the things I like the best about teaching college freshmen is watching them awaken. In early September, they're still children, trying to play children's games with their teachers; by November, many are wide-eyed with possibility. Amazed, they begin to realize that real study, real mastery of anything that matters, calls for effort beyond what they've ever dreamed—and the best of them begin along the path, flailingly at first, but then with surer and surer steps. One of my favorite images of such dawning awareness is graphic: a freshman composition student literally slapping her forehead and reminding herself, aloud, "This is *college*, Jenn!"

I love such awakenings in part because I remember mine so well, though it was long ago and far away from the life I live now. My own realization that I'd entered a new world at the university began not in the classrooms of my English major, but in college choir. From the start, choir at the University of Delaware was serious business. It was treated like a varsity sport. Freshmen were invited to choir camp two weeks before school began; they rehearsed with the choir and auditioned at a literal camp on the Chesapeake Bay, dislocated even from the campus they didn't yet know; they were watched coolly by the director, Joseph Huszti, and upperclassmen; and then, in the first week of school, asked to join Concert Choir—or not.

To this day, I'm not sure why I was invited to camp. My high school director must have written a very good letter. I had a pleasant enough voice, and I was obedient and serious and worked as hard as he asked—easy enough to do. But I hadn't even qualified for district chorus, and most of the other freshmen at Delaware's choir camp had been in *all-state*. I had never played a part with a name in a high school musical, had never been considered for solos in concerts. And the choir certainly didn't need sopranos.

But I think I know why I was invited to stay. During my tryout in the camp's dining hall, Mr. Huszti wheeled from the piano to face his graduate assistant. "This is a coloratura," he said, completely ignoring me, squinting past his assistant through the big windows to the sycamores quiet in the heat outside. "Though she has no idea." And, in fact, I didn't—I had to ask an upperclassman that afternoon what a coloratura *was*, and she regarded me with unconcealed skepticism as she answered. Only the next April, during a lesson, did I really grasp the nature of what had been prophesied for me, when I finally felt how to open my throat to make my upper airway (as I'd learned to call it by then) a sort of echo chamber. The oddest sound came out, nearly without effort—so high and vibrating in the back of my palate that it felt like it was floating out of my ears. Mr. Huszti whooped and brought people from other parts of the building as I dutifully repeated the sound over and over, easy when you know how. From then on, scores for twelve parts began to appear on our music stands, and my job was to make the ultra-high notes that soared above everyone else—static electricity rather than music. Up there, I was exempt from the exact diction expected of everyone else; I simply piped unearthly vowels. I felt like I existed in another dimension.

Nothing in my high school chorus experience had prepared me to imagine college choir. Mr. Huszti was intense and (it often seemed) obsessed, and he expected us to be the same. Everyone in the choir had a voice lesson at least once a week, a sectional practice twice a week, and whole-choir practice two afternoons a week from 4-6 p.m.—at least, we were supposed to stop at 6, but often we went over and had to run to the dining halls before they closed. We entered a self-contained world in that basement room in Old College Hall. Freshmen sometimes fidgeted and grumbled at the strangeness of our practice—but not for long, under the glares of the upperclassmen. We seemed to do very little of what I had thought choirs did—singing songs. We spent at least twenty minutes every rehearsal warming up, doing vocal drills and exercises, and we sometimes returned to that regime in mid-session. We practiced counting the crazy time signatures of our music, 7 with one hand, 8 with the other. When we did pick up a score, we almost always began in the middle, then worked oddly back and forth over sections. Only as we were approaching a concert did we sing anything through from start to finish. Often, we would simply practice one phrase, over and over—one night we worked on a page of Britten for an hour.

All of this drove home a clear lesson: being exact mattered. Freshmen who arrived with expressive theories of art were quickly disabused of them. Once, an earnest senior music major—a choir star—raised his hand and described a revisionist recorded version he had just bought of the piece that we were rehearsing. Could we try that tempo? he asked. The explosion was swift. "If Schubert had wanted it sung allegro, he would have written allegro!" Mr. Huszti shouted. "Why would a composer bother to write, if you could do it any way you wanted? Your obligation as a musician is to read the music! Otherwise, what are you . . .?" He paused, searching for a sufficiently insulting term. "An interpreter!" he spat. No one asked again.

We spent hours on precise pronunciation—not just of the German and Latin and Italian we sang, but also of the English. We practiced ending and beginning consonants over and over—how to make them clear without seeming prissy. Given the variety of discordant upstate Delaware, southern Jersey and suburban Philadelphia dialects that we brought, Mr. Huszti faced continual trials. "Ghao," he'd sneer when we sang "go" in our native tongues, or "There may well be bombs in Gilead, but this song is not about them."

All of this exactitude didn't exclude feeling from our music-making—indeed, it was the other pole that defined our work. To add energy to our singing, we were instructed to count beats up, not down (which I still do when I hear music sung or played with spirit). We were taught, too, to sway and move as we sang—newcomers who stood still were chided until they became fluid or fled. This dancing to inner voices, along with Mr. Huszti's directive that we open our mouths *wide* when we sang, led to predictable hooting when we visited local high schools, an unpleasant experience for freshmen who still suspected that this way of performing was eccentric. But no one was more eccentric than Mr. Huszti himself. With his reading glasses low on his nose (how did he keep them from falling off?), he'd sometimes sway so hard that we were afraid that he'd fall off the podium; when he was frustrated or moved, he'd run his hand back through his thin black hair, tearing at it, and then forget and leave it standing straight up. My high school choir director, with his placid conducting, seemed far away.

The music itself was difficult and strange: lots of early twentieth-century things, many romantic period works, remarkable sixteenth-century masses. Mr. Huszti's favorites seemed to be Britten, whom I learned to love, and Schumann, whom I still can't stand. With late-adolescent carelessness, I seldom registered the titles of the music that we performed; we were usually told simply to "Take out the Vaughan Williams," or "Go to the Mozart." Only as I have aged and have married a man who is careful about things like concerto numbers am I beginning to appreciate our enormous repertoire. "Oh, I sang *that*," I'll say as a new CD plays. "You sang the Berlioz *Requiem*?" my husband will ask, incredulous—and, indeed, we did. I've always remembered the titles of the things I liked best, though. My favorite might be the Britten *St. Nicholas*—where I was a Pickled Boy and sang the unearthly alleluias from the back balcony—but I also remember in particular the music which took as its text poems that we were reading in my literature classes: settings of the Whitman *Carols of Death* and Blake's *Songs of Innocence and Experience*.

We did work on less exalted ground, of course—even Mr. Huszti had to recognize that concerts performed for parents and college administrators had to have some "regular" music. We sang "Oklahoma" and "If I Loved You"—giving probably the most precise renditions of these numbers ever performed. We sang some wonderful middlebrow music—spirituals, for instance, where we had great fun with tone and tempo. When we moved to really low-rent pieces, they were always treated cavalierly. We sight-read ordinary Christmas carols only once as a group before our Christmas concerts, in dress rehearsal, and we often sang the Delaware "Fight Song" and "Alma Mater" at football games without practicing them at all. Despite these concessions, there were lines that Mr. Huszti wouldn't cross. Most memorably, when we sang *The Messiah*, we stopped at the real end of the Christmas section, concluding with "His Yoke Is Easy." Our parents sat, puzzled, waiting for the other shoe to drop—but of course we weren't singing the "Hallelujah Chorus" out of order. "Didn't you have enough time to practice it?" my mother asked.

Many nights in the basement of Old College, such discipline, such puritanism, grated on my soul. Why *couldn't* we, for once, sing something straight through, I'd wonder; why couldn't we sing more music that was fun and familiar? Why did we have to keep going over and over sections that seemed perfectly fine? One night, I was caught outright in such a mood; I hadn't realized that my body oozed frustration, but it clearly did. "Be patient, Susan," Mr. Huszti said, out of the blue. "Not everyone is as smart as you are." I froze, horrified, as others wheeled to see what had caused this outburst. That was the only time in my life that I've been called on such mental behavior, though I've deserved it much more often.

On other nights, though, there was no need to chastise me or anyone else, for time stopped as the rehearsal took on its own energy, and getting this phrase, this section right seemed the most crucial work in the world. Those nights, I bristled when we moved on without quite finishing. Now and then, too, magic happened—the music soared as everything came together, and the notes plaited and separated and braided back together, and we held our breaths when we were done. It hardly mattered that the concerts to follow were anticlimaxes—we'd risen once to the music, we knew, and that was the important thing.

The end of my college choir career came quietly: I left of my own accord after the first semester of my junior year. I remember no special effort to persuade me to stay nor any particular goodbye—possibly another child with the gift for those static electric sounds had emerged at choir camp. The choir was planning to tour Europe the next summer; I was getting married in July. I told Mr. Huszti that I didn't have the financial resources, the time, or the energy to go along, and I simply didn't register for choir in the spring. In fact, this was an excuse, for I could have worked my wedding date around the tour, and my parents probably would have been glad to subsidize me. My actual reason for leaving seemed much harder for me to explain at the time: I had discovered that my real gift was with words, not music. By then, the professors in my English classes were treating me as Mr. Huszti treated the stars in the choir, and books opened themselves to me easily as music seemed to open itself to them. At the time, I was afraid that Mr. Huszti would be angry at me for throwing away all the effort that he'd spent building my voice; now I know that I was foolish, for he, of all people, would have understood vocation.

That was the end of my serious singing. Into my mid-thirties, I could still make the coloratura sound—a parlor trick at the end. Now my voice has lowered to alto, and I'm finding the easy depths of the chest voice that was such a trial for me at nineteen. I still use my voice lessons after a fashion, nearly thirty years later. I read in church, I teach, I run meetings, I give presentations—and, in doing all of these, I'm glad for the way I learned to make soft words carry, for the way I can catch others with my tone and help them see what I'd like them to see. I sing, too, with my Girl Scouts. Moms coming early enough to find us in our final circle say, "You have such a *wonderful* voice," and I smile and thank them—though I know that, compared to *real* musicians, my singing voice is finally just pleasant.

My most important legacies from college choir, it turns out, have nothing to do with my voice. There I began to learn what it meant to teach; there I began to be able to imagine the life that I have since created for myself, a life spent in colleges, with others on the verge of awakening to themselves. And, perhaps most significantly of all, there I began to learn what it meant to lose oneself in creating something, as time and space disappear and work becomes all that matters.

The best of my memories of college choir shine with such absorption, for, in them, we are sitting in that basement room in Old College, semicircles of chairs facing Mr. Huszti. Over and over a phrase we sing, breaking to his signals of frustration and starting again, until suddenly we get it right. Mr. Huszti grins and says simply, "Fine; now take out the Bach," and we begin again with another phrase—until suddenly the practice is over, and I stumble out into the dark blue of a Delaware spring evening, heavy with magnolia, or into the dark, wet breeze of a Delaware fall night, knowing I'll have to rush to dinner and not caring. On such nights, I began to see what it might mean to be a college student. On those nights, too, I began to glimpse a world informed by expectations that would stretch me into someone I would hardly recognize, until I became myself a taskmaster, an eccentric, a preparer of the way for magic.

Eleven

THE BEAUTY HORSE
(1996)

SHE WAITS FOR ME every morning at the gate of her pasture, just this side of the cattleguard that marks the national forest boundary. Sometimes she stretches when she sees me coming around the curve of the road on my morning run, her short cocoa legs and stocky golden brown body extended in an exaggerated waking cat pull, black mane tossed out of her eyes. I've been giving her daily treats for almost two years now, sweet carrots from the farmers' market and new fall apples when I can, supermarket versions when I can't, always sugar.

This winter, her owner was bringing hay one day when I passed, and I learned that her name is Meg. I've been calling her the Beauty Horse for so long, though, that I still think of her that way, though it's such a silly kid name. I noticed her a long time before I met her, and I felt sorry for her—she lived alone down in her opulent meadow by the Mink Creek, and I learned from my friend Anne that horses were happiest with company. One day, the Beauty Horse was at the gate when I passed, and I spoke to her; the next, she let me touch her neck before she shied away. I started bringing her treats then, but she was wary. Some days, she eyed me for a long time until she snatched the apple from my hand and fled. When she did stand still, we were both inept at the handoffs—sugar cubes hopelessly vanishing in the snow, carrots in the mud, apples bounding under sagebrush. Some days, she didn't come at all, staying off by the creek, down in the grass. For weeks, I would think that she didn't like me.

Slowly, though, we've learned each other, and now she looks for my coming. Some mornings, when her owners have shut her off in the north part of the pasture, we have to do a Romeo and Juliet act to meet, for that field is down a steep bank from the road. She can reach my hand in only one place, and I have to squat carefully on the slippery bitterbrush roots and grass and reach my hand through the barbed wire, while she climbs her front legs up the rocky bank and stretches her neck to reach the tips of my fingers. This is risky when it's rainy or snowy, and we've both slipped, but I always manage to pass her something. Our favorite place is the gate, where we can pet, for now she lets me stroke her neck and even kiss her muzzle between the eyes, and she nuzzles me under the arm. When I miss a few days, she misses me—after this spring's break, when I was gone a week, she ran and capered when she saw me, and even managed a sort of middle-aged rear.

Anne thought at first that she was a special rare kind of horse, with her creme brulee color and thick, short shape, but I've learned now from her owner that she's just a regular Morgan mare. Her intelligence, though, seems to go way beyond the usual. One day, when I was slow getting the goods, she reached through the gate, took the big zipper of my parka in her teeth, and unzipped the pocket where I always carry her food.

I wish that the Beauty Horse had more chance to show her disposition. Her owner takes her for walks or rides her now and then, but he works and has no children, so most of the time she's left to amuse herself. Her pasture is more West Virginia than Kentucky, with its assortment of old tractors, camper parts, and scrap lumber that someone is planning to use sometime. She has no shelter, gets shaggy in winter and curly soaked in rain, and her mane mats with burrs in summer into punk spikes that stay for weeks. She seems content, though, drinking from the creek, hay and grass and flowers to eat. She has a shady bower of trees, plenty of room, and, in this spring season, the gentle pour of meadowlark song and angry *phoebe!* calls of oversexed chickadees to remind her that there are other beings in the world.

The first winter that we were friends, I dreamed of buying her, of freeing her from her solitude. Anne had room at her place, I thought, with only three other horses, and I could pay to board the Beauty Horse. I could ride her, quiet afternoons in the hills, just the two of us; I could see that her mane was never matted. On Christmas day, I woke up pouting and wondered why. Then I realized that I had hoped that someone would buy her for me—that someone would know how much I wanted her, though I'd never suggested such a thing.

But even before the turkey was cool, I acknowledged that this was nonsense. Though I loved the idea of horses as a child, read the *Black Stallion* books (even the obscure ones about the Sulky Colt) and rode my share of sticks around the yard, my life had been empty of real horses. The Beauty Horse, in fact, is the first one I have ever really known. The few times I've ridden have been unpleasant, to say the least. As an adolescent, once or twice at summer camp, I bounced along on trail rides, amazed at how far I was off the ground, trying not to whimper. The only time I've ridden as an adult was on Anne's big, raw Foxie, who insisted on trotting briskly straight down the sides of canyons with me clinging so hard to the saddlehorn that I could barely unfold my thumbs the next day. Plus, I know nothing about caring for them, their ailments, their grooming, their feeding, all of the mysterious leathery accoutrements that litter their barns. I've heard horror stories about horses blowing up with wind, having to have their bellies slit, getting chills and dying from not being wiped off properly. How many disasters could happen if the Beauty Horse were mine! What if she got sick? What if I did something wrong and killed her? More likely, but no less distressingly, what if she didn't want to be ridden? If she rejected me? If I had to struggle with her, to try to dominate her, to change her, or, what if she won and I grew angry and we came to hate each other? What if she ended up more alone, more unhappy than she was now—in *my* pasture? And where was all that time that I was going to spend with her going to come from, after all—I who feel guilty now because I don't have time to play with my cats every day.

So, my common sense and my heart tell me, things are better this way—we only see the best in each other now; we're not responsible for each other. She's the sweet being who lights my mornings with her gentle nudges; I'm the bringer of treats who never imposes. She never sees my impatience, my nervousness; I never see her will and her temper. To borrow from Keats: this way, she will always be fair for me, and I hope that I will always be fair for her.

Lately, it has occurred to me that I have been gathering other Beauty Horses in my life, other places where I have made my peace with just visiting. I feed wild birds, though I know that some fall day the swallows and hummingbirds will vanish. I have casual friends. I teach my students without learning the anguished details of their private lives. I freelance, writing one or two articles for a magazine and then doing something else. I sit for a while on a volunteer board, then move on to another. In an especially joyful part of my life, every other week and one weekend a month, I borrow fourteen young girls from their parents for Brownie meetings. With adolescence safely a few years in the distance, so far we have been always fair for each other, too—I'm the person who always has something fun to do, the person who takes them skiing and rock climbing and camping and walking in the autumn woods, the person with infinite crayons and no life that doesn't include them on those afternoons. I discipline them only slightly; I listen to them always; I don't get grumpy. In turn, they give me their best, too—their mothers marvel at how little they whine at Scouts, how willing they are to try things, how they're learning to share, how cheerful they are.

We're cheating, of course, the Brownies and I—living in a fairy tale where we're all on our best behavior, dodging the irritations, the clashes, the dark sides that people have to deal with when they commit to the dailies. Irresponsible? My younger self would certainly have said so. When I was in my twenties and thirties, I couldn't let anything alone. Flirtations led at least to imagined consummations, sometimes to literal ones, and almost always to anguished psychodrama. I couldn't sit on a committee without imagining how I'd run it better; I couldn't see a request for proposals without yearning to apply; I couldn't make a friend without baring my soul and expecting the same in return.

Slowly, though, I learned that trying to own everything wouldn't work. Some things I just couldn't do as well as the other people who were already doing them. Some things I made worse for trying. Some things were hopeless in the first place. And sometimes having to cope with the reality of other people ruined the good things I could do for them; and, when they found my flaws, they lost their joy in me. Casual friends can give each other things too, I learned—the cheerful sense of being liked, the comforting assurance of finite expectations. Sometimes, I think, we need just to give each other a break, to let people play at being their best for us, to imagine what life might be like if we could be forever what we can sometimes temporarily be.

So these days, I'm making my peace with distance. I *am* proud of myself for the times that I have mastered the dailies and have learned to live with less-than-perfect things. I'm proud, for instance, that I've finally become really married, and that I've ridden the ups and downs of having the same job in the same place for almost twenty years. But I'm also proud of just visiting sometimes, of finding unapologetic, irresponsible joy in the song of a bird I'll never have to take to the vet, in the bright smiles of children not mine, in the Beauty Horse, waiting every morning at the gate.

Twelve

ANGELS AT THE DOOR
(1998)

AMONG THE MOST POPULAR characters in Mormon folklore in the Intermountain West, where I live today, are the Nephites. The Nephites—three aged, odd, often bearded or gaunt strangers, part Ancient Mariner, part Cain—were said in the nineteenth and early twentieth centuries to appear without warning at people's doors. In these stories, Nephites sometimes arrive as a group, sometimes singly, coming at inopportune times of illness, poverty, personal crisis for residents. They make people nervous, with their eccentric look and apparent indigence. They always ask for help. Surprisingly, given that Nephites' characteristic posture in those doorways might fairly be described as "lurking," the people approached in the stories passed down to us are always charitable. They share their already meager dinners or their clothing; they warm the strangers at their fires and provide beds on howling nights; they listen to tales of woe in the midst of their own travail. Then, after the Nephites leave, something wonderful happens, the miracle solving just the specific trial that the household was facing. A child wakes with her fever broken; the cupboard is filled with finest flour; a check for exactly the amount needed for homestead fees is discovered on the kitchen table. Hundreds of stories about Nephites have been recorded, and the appeal of this theme apparently continues, for even into the late twentieth century people attest that they've met Nephites who were stranded with flat tires on the highway, left without luggage at the airport, rewarding the improbably kind.

Though it's tempting to smile at such accounts of anonymous and deserved reward as wishful thinking, I know better: I know that such unannounced chances to prove one's worth still exist. In fact, I *was* a sort of Nephite, though in a diminished genre and with a mercifully brief career. In the early 1990s, after I had placed some freelance essays with *Gourmet* magazine, the editors hired me to write two travel feature articles, sending me to the Adirondacks and the Maine coast. Along with constructing dream-vacation narratives, my duties included anonymously reviewing restaurants and inns. At first, this seemed like fun. It certainly conferred power. In letter after letter to the editor, *Gourmet*'s readers insisted that the magazine served as a Bible for their travels, dictating every stop. I knew, thus, that a favorable mention could spell success for the deserving, while omission spelled a seriously missed opportunity (for in those days *Gourmet* writers did not critique the inferior or uninspired, but simply maintained discreet and tactful silence). How nice it would be to be able to help make the fortunes of people who did right by the apparently ordinary visitor. What fun finally to be able to exact some revenge on the people who did shoddy or pretentious work. I had been waiting all my life for such a chance.

In practice, though, much to my surprise, I ended up pitying the failures: salmon which was *not* "just out of the water," as had been promised; waiters who recommended bland chardonnay because I was a woman dining alone, who defined "au poivre" without waiting to be asked; chicken breasts stuffed with peppers and goat cheese and drizzled with artful yin-yang swirls of tomato/cilantro concasse but baked to a leathery crisp; rooms in stenciled duck bed and breakfasts where all available surfaces were so covered with knickknacks that there was no room for contact lens fluid.... Normally such things would have irritated or outraged me. But on these trips they just made me sad. Maybe the cook had slipped this once, I would find myself thinking as I chewed away; maybe I had just happened to choose the worst dish on the menu. The owner of this inn had spent so much time decorating it, and she was trying so hard. Who could guess what personal crisis had made that waitress so preoccupied, so inept? What made that waiter so rude?

I was a responsible reporter, and I never, thank heavens, had to pan the disappointing places. But I found myself increasingly wrapped in grief as I drove away from the failures, and their faces stayed in my memory long after the smiles of the fortunate receded.

So I wasn't sorry when, busy with other projects, I stopped writing query letters to *Gourmet*, and the editors stopped calling me. It was a relief to be able to eat a crummy meal again and be simply and personally miffed. But the damage to my innocence was done—for I began wondering about all of the potential angels in disguise that I had turned from my own door, and continued to turn away every day. Mormons don't tell stories about Nephites repulsed—how would you know that they were Nephites if you flunked?—but we are clearly meant to imagine them, the norm tacitly posed against the tales of virtue rewarded. What about the time that I looked up from grading a last student paper a few minutes before class to see a young man standing in my office door, asking, "Are you the secretary?"—wanting directions to the Business Building—and bit his head off? What about the supermarket clerk I frosted when she spent a long time chatting with the person in front of me while I fumed, late again? What about the people in traffic I pulled in front of, or the doddering stranger who smiled at me on the street whom I didn't greet out of pure obstinacy? What about the editing job I rushed, the present I picked out too hastily, the student conference where I lost interest? Any of them could have held blessings for me. Not just "blessings" as in divine lottery tickets—but potential for doing real good by another human being, chances to show the kindness in my heart, chances gone.

What happens if a Nephite comes on a bad day—when one is late for class or has argued with the beloved in the morning, or simply is grumpy? Is that it? Are Nephites, like anonymous *Gourmet* reporters, instructed to shake the dust from their feet and move on, inexorably and finally, when they meet the truly hopeless? If so, I'm afraid that we're all doomed—that those people in the stories exist only to make us guilty. Even if we do succeed in overcoming our selfishness, our nastiness, sometimes we will be ground down, no matter what we do, by sorrow and worry and fear for ourselves and those we love. It's hard to find patience for a stranger when one has just given, for days and days. It's very difficult to work always at the top of one's capacity, when others have asked and asked and asked, and one is simply tired. It's almost impossible to love when one feels unloved. The only way we can live and be sane, I've learned to believe, is to be a little selfish, a little lazy sometimes, and to forgive ourselves for that. But if the great test comes when we're caught in depression or feeling pressed beyond all measure, surely there's no hope for us. Like the people whose encounters with Nephites are not recorded, and the people with the tired salmon and puckery wine, most of us will live our lives quietly, a little sadly, wondering why we've never had the chance to prove ourselves when in fact that chance has come and gone.

And yet, I can't help hoping that God understands. For we're supposed to be made in his image, and, despite all of our petty meanness, we can also transcend ourselves. I've seen the amazing compassion that people do extend to each other—not all the time, or even very often—but sometimes, in moments of blinding grace. I've seen people set quarrels aside and rebuild friendships; I've seen people reform, for real. I've felt my own heart forgive. And I've seen my own pity swell, against all logic, triumphing over the petty revenge I'd planned, about something as trivial as wilted lettuce, about something as important as anger. If *we* can do this, how could an angel do less? Surely this compassion in us isn't a dead end; surely it echoes something beyond us, giving us hope that, in spite of all the selfishness of which we are capable, we will be allowed to show ourselves at our best. Surely we will have a second chance, and a third, and a seventy-times-seventh, and, eventually, we will shine, surprising ourselves, earning what's been waiting for us all along.

When I was a child, I thought that the line in the Lord's Prayer that says "Forgive us our trespasses, as we forgive those who trespass against us" was a threat. I imagined a cosmic double column accounting system, where we would only be granted the exact compassion that we granted others. Lately, though, I've been wondering if that line is meant as a reassurance instead—a reminder that, because we *do* forgive each other even in our humanness, we can serve for each other as a faint prefiguring of the opening arms ahead.

I hope so. At any rate, I know that I must believe that the Nephites shake their heads in sadness as they walk away from a farm house at the foot of the Wasatch or the Big Lost River Mountains or the San Rafael Swell, turning to look back at its isolated light burning in the dusk. In my version of the stories, they know that the person who just snapped at them and closed the door can think only of that sick child, or they know that, with wife gone, farm apparently soon to be, simply continuing is triumph enough. I must believe that Nephites never gloat, that they only weep for the poor human creatures who have lost this chance at the gifts they bear. And I must believe, most of all, that sooner or later another knock will sound on that door—a knock announcing, once more, the possibility of grace, again, an angel at the door.

Thirteen

MY FATHER'S WORK
(1989)

My next-younger brother loves the home movies that my father took of us as children. He has copied them into videotaped anthologies, which he and his wife watch often, giggling about how silly we were, and he shows these tapes at family parties, where they are apparently great hits. He has even sent me copies—me, the wanderer who, inexplicably in his mind, lives in Idaho, so far away from the family. I cannot watch those movies. The images of Christmas mornings, especially, take me back to moments that are awkward to remember—moments when I stood frozen with my brother in the paralyzing glare of the light bar over my father's Bell and Howell movie camera as I stumbled down the steps to inspect my stocking, left blinded when the lights went out. "Do something," my smiling and exasperated father would order us as the camera ran on. "Don't just stand there!" And we'd try—but in those movies we look to me like bad child actors impersonating happy children on Christmas morning, artificial and posed.

That Christmas morning scene is an emblem of the way that I felt about my father himself for many years. Though he was a sweet man, a good and loving man, he was never quite at ease somehow. In social situations and at ritual times like holidays and vacations, he often appeared so awkward that he seemed like a bad actor himself. As a child, I watched other people's fathers—always so substantial and relaxed in their roles—and marveled.

When I grew to be an adolescent, and for a long time afterwards, I pitied my father, and I blamed his work for the way that he was, for it seemed to me the sort of supremely gray occupation that would kill spontaneity and make a man feel that he was somehow less than real. I noticed that others described their fathers' work using concrete nouns: machine operators, or teachers, or salesmen. When we spoke at home of my father's occupation, in contrast, we called it, simply and generically, "work." In fact, he was an accountant, then comptroller and secretary-treasurer for a company that made coffee vending machines. The duties that he performed were incomprehensible to me as a child, though my father's place of work itself was very interesting. In one bittersweet smelling part of the operation, workers transformed raw coffee beans to the brown powder that went between thin tissue-paper sheets to became a series of continuous machine-sized coffee bags, strips that looked like ribbons of giant ravioli. Other workers assembled the vending machines themselves from delicate electrical parts which my brother and I always eyed with great curiosity but were instructed strictly not to touch when we went "up to work" with my father on Sunday afternoons.

All that I could tell about Daddy's own work was that it seemed to be boring. He appeared to spend his days entering numbers on a metal adding machine, working with others in a beige room crowded with dull green metal desks and smelling of industrial floor-tile polish. Later, when I was in college and he was secretary-treasurer, he had his own office, but it still looked drab to me. He also seemed to work more than anyone else. He never arrived home before six, though his office was only a ten-minute drive away. Just about every night, he brought work home with him; after dinner he'd take it down to his little office off the rec room, shut the door, turn on the Phillies for company, and stay there until after we went to bed. He often spent part of Saturday, Sunday, or both, at the office. The only time that he didn't work was during our annual two-week summer vacation. My mother's constant lament as we were growing up was that the company exploited him—but I always understood that he worked this way by choice, seeing the tasks that had to be done, and believing that he was the one to do them.

When I first read Russian literature as a freshman in college, I thought that I recognized him as a Chekhov clerk, and the pathos of that image stayed with me for years. He certainly did lead the respectable, regulated life of those clerks. Every working day, he came home for lunch and ate a predictable meal: leftovers from dinner or a coldcut sandwich, chips, and half a blueberry or apple Tasteypie. He never drank; he never smoked. He and my mother would occasionally have friends over for an evening when I was little, but even that dwindled away by the time that I was in high school. They did go to the Presbyterian Church every week, where my father's role echoed his work life: he was the elder who did more work than anyone else, and he was the church treasurer, managing its books and counting the collection himself.

Our recreation, too, was regulated. When my next-younger brother and I were little, my family took vacation road trips, always in the first two weeks of August. We went to "interesting" places—Niagara Falls, Florida, Canada, New England—but these were *not* adventures. My mother wrote months ahead for motel brochures, and our day-by-day itinerary was always carefully arranged. After my parents had two more children and our family was too big and too diverse in age for comfortable travel, we went to "the shore" (either Cape Cod or New Jersey), and we always rented the same houses. Holidays, too, were fixed in tradition: we were always filmed coming downstairs on Christmas morning; every Easter we searched for our Easter baskets; we always went to the same Fourth of July parade and sat in the same block. Though I enjoyed these rituals as a child, after I left home I was sorry that even the celebrations of my father's life were utterly predictable.

My father also shared the frugality of Chekhov's clerks. He earned a good salary but pumped most of it into insurance, savings, and very, very safe investments. Though I knew that we were richer than most of my friends, we lived poorer, except for our comfortable home on an acre. We drove Chevies and kept them until their odometers registered hundreds of thousands of miles. All of our clothes came from Sears, to my adolescent embarrassment as my friends wore Villager sweaters and John Wanamaker shoes. We bought store brands at the grocery store. It wasn't that my father deprived us—we received wonderful presents at Christmas and birthdays—it was just that we were very careful all the time. Money was an awkward subject at our house, something impolite to mention. Again, in my young adulthood, I blamed my father's work for this: he was paid to pinch pennies at work, I reasoned, and so he was compulsive about frugality at home.

For a long time, thus, my father (and his work, for it was impossible for me to tell where one ended and the other began) seemed very sad. My attitude was fed by the ethos of the decade in which I became a young adult, for we learned to believe that work should make a difference somehow. I just couldn't see, back in 1970, that my father's work mattered, except for helping his bosses get richer. In my twenties and early thirties, I fell prey to the snobberies of the time and tried to avoid telling anyone what my father did. I devoutly wished that he'd been a carpenter, a farmer, a doctor, a violinist, even a factory worker. As an accountant's daughter, I had no right either to reverse snobbery or to the comfort of belonging. My father seemed to be part of a group that I heard people alternately criticizing and condescending to: a bourgeois drone who was missing what was important, what was joyful because he was obsessed with security and devoted to a meaningless job. I didn't spend much time with my father in those years. Though this was partly because I had moved away, I also felt that I had to reinvent myself, to break free of his well-ordered and terribly self-conscious life.

This was the low point in our relationship—a low point about which I held my peace at the time, to my great relief now. Since then, I've learned some things about my father that have tempered my pity with pride. In the last few years, in fact, I have realized that his well-ordered life was a victory for him. And, I have realized that I was right when I thought that he acted like a role-player himself, for he was reinventing John Hendricks as surely as I reinvented myself in my twenties and early thirties.

He never talked about his family to me, so, when I began to recognize that he was growing older and to wish for more closeness with him, I wrote and asked about his youth. He wrote back, and I supplemented what I learned with talks with my mother. What I learned changed everything. My father was the oldest son of a printer, a second-generation German immigrant. The family lived in a neighborhood on the edge of the city, a respectable working-class place, in a house right up against the railroad tracks. When my father was an adolescent, his own father suddenly died, from an illness whose exact nature I've never been able to learn, except that it was very ordinary. My grandfather had no insurance and very little money in the bank; he left a wife, my father, and two younger children. His improvidence caused them very hard times. My grandmother, a big, strong German woman named Lena, went to work cooking at school cafeterias. In summer, she worked at a camp for rich children in the Poconos, where she arose before dawn to bake bread and to haul huge pots of stew and soup. She apparently worked continuously, crushingly, and uncomplainingly.

To help, my father took odd jobs while he was in high school. Then, as soon as he could, he assumed the responsibility for supporting his family, with what I now recognize as the absolute and guilty responsibility of an eldest child. He chose, in a gesture which I also recognize now, a profession that was the antithesis of his father's: a secure job, with no layoffs, no possibility of injury, and all sorts of opportunities for financial security. To get to that job, he put himself through Drexel in a work-study program, bolstering family finances as he earned his degree. As soon as he could, he passed his C.P.A. exam. He grew up to be all the things that his father wasn't: a white-collar worker responsible about money; a dependable provider for his family who insured that his wife would never have to work if he died; owner of a big split-level house in a nice suburb. So, in fact, he *was* acting a little on those long-ago Christmas mornings, aware that he was living a life that he had invented for himself.

His life was marked by several testimonials to his success in creating this persona. When I was about eight, his bosses went bankrupt. The problem was evidently not in the company itself but in how the bosses managed the profits; I remember them as being two high-livers who authored a glossy cookbook, and once, learning that I was crazy about horses, let us use their box at Devon for a night. These bosses were banished, and the company went into receivership. One would think that, with finances in a mess, the new bosses would have fired the accountants and started over. But they retained my father, admiring the policies that he'd tried to convince the first bosses to use. Absolving him of responsibility for the downfall, they promoted him to treasurer.

I was present at another triumph. He died soon after his retirement, of a cancer detected within months of the day that he left the company—suggesting that the link between him and his work was not just of my imagination. When I traveled east for his funeral, I was afraid that few people would attend—isn't that what happens to Chekhov clerks? But the church was full of people who all wanted to shake my hand and talk about him. Many of them were co-workers: secretaries, younger accountants, bosses, even one of the deposed partners from long ago, shabbily resplendent still in a fur-collared coat. Some of them had tears in their eyes; all had loved him. The company's vice-president, a very old acquaintance, pressed my hand in silence, then smiled sadly. "Your father," he said, "was a gentleman. He was the last of the gentlemen." And that afternoon completed my realization that my father, in his drudgery-filled job, whose life seemed so sadly fixed and paranoically responsible, had become, indeed, a gentleman—a man of his word, a man one could trust, always and absolutely.

One of the hardest lessons of my maturity has been realizing that I have no right to pity my father, no right to regret the unglamorous bourgeois steadiness in which we lived. Yes, those Christmas-morning movies are still painful. I wish that he'd talked to us more and photographed us less. But I realize now that we were one more indication that he'd succeeded in what he was driven to do—four secure children, three of whom finished college. My father must have realized at some point that this life that he'd made for his family wasn't going to come apart at the seams, even if something happened to him. That must have been a proud moment for him.

I don't altogether like the legacy that he's left me, especially the attitude toward work. I'm often in my office before the secretary, and I leave late; sometimes I work on weekends. I think, too, that I alone am the one who must do things if they are to be done right. But, though I still wish that I could be less driven than my father, I've realized that I don't need to pity him anymore. For I'm the daughter of a man who held the world together single-handedly in the quiet of his own mind, at work and at home. Ultimately, it doesn't matter what the work was; it was honorably done, and the most important thing is what it meant to him. Though I have no wish to live his life, I see now that it was every bit as triumphant as I could ever wish my own to be.

Fourteen

THE FIREBABE
(1998)

I AM A MOST UNLIKELY FIREFIGHTER. I have feared fire since I was six, thanks to a particularly gruesome *Dragnet* episode about arson. When Yellowstone burned, I could not watch the news, the images of flames crowning high in the air, the awful rush of fire through the trees. But, at 44, a teacher, writer, and Girl Scout leader with plenty of other things to do, I find myself a member of a volunteer fire department in the rural Intermountain West. My mother, my students, and my friends are impressed. Actually, it is a decision of cowardice. When we move out from town to the edge of the national forest, Ford asks about fire protection, and our real estate agent is a volunteer. He easily enlists Ford, a volunteer in his youth and later, before we met. "We also have many ladies in the department," the agent says, looking at me significantly. "We believe that women can do anything that men can." "Of course she'll help," Ford replies proudly. "She's like that." Not knowing what to say, I say yes.

"*Everybody's* afraid of fire," smiles the man giving us nomex uniforms when I confess, *sotto voce*, hoping to be disqualified. I know then that I am in the company of very brave people, or lunatics. The veteran firefighters are an oddly assorted lot, but they have one thing in common: they seem to welcome fires, complaining of a summer when the department hasn't had enough calls to "stay sharp." Many are retired military men. The department also has a cadre of energetic, can-do-style middle-aged men into which Ford immediately fits, including Paul, a former technical writing student of mine at the university, Bob, our trainer, and Matt, a superb mechanic and perhaps the best firefighter in the group. Most of the women are also older, ex-combat nurses and such—long veterans of the department. Only Peggy and Kim, social work students in their late thirties and relatively new firefighters, seem at all like me. Even they are clearly tougher. Kim has spent a lot of time jumping out of airplanes, and Peggy, married to a railroader, takes no guff, despite a glamorous exterior that I later discover occasionally includes coming to fires in mascara and wearing her heavies over lace nighties. The other woman our age, Lorraine, Matt's wife, is in another category completely. Large, a little rough in her humor and speech, mother of three teenagers, Lorraine seems to regard our one modern truck, the Quick Response Unit, as her personal property. She offers her opinions with conviction at meetings and has good grounds for those opinions, I soon realize, for she is evidently first to every fire. "Does she sleep in her uniform?" Kim wonders aloud during a break in a meeting, and Peggy and I dissolve in unfirefighter-like giggles. This is the year that the "Sportsbabe" is new on the radio—another big, blunt, no-fooling competent woman—and we begin to refer to Lorraine as "the firebabe" among ourselves.

In my last preliminary training session, I realize that I differ from everyone else in another way. I am perhaps even more afraid of our engines than of fire itself. I have never driven anything larger than a full-sized pick-up truck, and the idea of jouncing many feet above the ground in the company of thousands of pounds of shifting water is unappealing, to say the least. The department's two regular engines are aging, quirky in the gears and steering, covered with dials and pressure gauges that look ready to explode at any moment. Indeed, before I take my trial drive, it is impressed on me how easily one could set something wrong and wreck the engine. The tanker truck—a bona fide antique—is even worse, and, when Ford proves that he is among the few competent to drive it, cheers erupt. Seeking no such glory,

I am allowed to test drive Engine 2, with Paul as my amused instructor. While I do complete the quarter mile drive successfully, and even turn the thing around somehow, my performance is such that no one complains when I manage always to be second or third to the station, always a passenger.

Despite my hopes that the department will never have another fire, the very day after Ford and I are official, we are called to one of the most dramatic fires that anyone remembers. While much of our district consists of what firefighters call the "urban interface," an area where houses encroach on national forest and BLM land, it also includes a stretch of four-lane interstate highway and a nasty light industrial strip just outside the city limits—a zone of junkyards and recycling plants and ancient trailer parks. My first fire is on that strip, in a dilapidated salvage yard whose levels of deposit reach nearly to the fossil record. When we come around the corner from our canyon and look across the greater valley to see the oily black column of smoke towering hundreds of feet high, flames visible five miles away, I know that I would turn the car home if I were alone, mailing my uniform back. Ford says "Holy shit!"—and speeds up.

It is a horrible afternoon. BLM, Forest Service, and city trucks are already on the scene helping us, thanks to a cooperative agreement for large fires that I will have cause to bless repeatedly in the months ahead. And I am never personally in danger—the department realizes what it has in me, and I am relegated to warning people not to linger under live overhead power lines. But what I see convinces me that I will never be able to fight fires. The junkyard is full of paint and bullets and exploding cars; the noise and smell are debilitating. It is all that I can do not to run away. My worst moment comes when I am directed to take water to people on the line, and see Ford and Peggy in the doorway of a shed, hosing down a smoking car. "What are you doing?" I yell, and they turn to me, baffled.

The next afternoon, we fight another fire, this one started by children playing with matches in the sagebrush. The fire is just one canyon over from ours, and it is gaining on a house as we arrive. Ford immediately joins Bob, Matt, Lorraine, and the BLM crews defending the house from its green lawn, a wonderful firebreak. I play the role of handmaiden again. At the height of the action, when I am dispensing canteens, an all-female BLM crew goes by on a little brush unit even niftier than Lorraine's Q.R. They are slim and muscular and 25; they are grinning through the smoke and talking as if they were on their way to the mall. The only word to describe them, I realize, is "firebabes." I feel useless.

After the fire is knocked down and the home saved, I am dispatched with our littlest hose to work with BLM crews mopping up the burned-over area. While they chop at smoldering patches, turning over hot ant hills and opening the roots around sagebrush, I bleat the hose at random sparks to prevent flare-ups. I am hot and tired and absolutely drained after these two days, wondering how I will ever be able to stand this. "Let's hope that this is *it* for a while," I say.

The nearest BLM crew member, a cheerful man in his late twenties, looks up and utters one of the most shocking things that I've ever heard. "Black trees make green wallets," he grins, and I glimpse another world.

Two hours later, showered and in a sundress, I'm standing behind our house watering our lawn. The tiny hose echoes the one I handled earlier, and I wiggle my bare feet in the cool wet grass. I think about the xeriscaping advice we got when we moved out here, the surprise of our ecologically correct friends when Ford started carrying in sod, 45-pound roll by 45-pound roll, to make this little patch between us and the junipers and sagebrush. A monarch butterfly stops to drink from a grass blade near me. At this moment, a green lawn is the most beautiful thing in the world.

We never again have two such intense days piled back to back. But we have plenty to do. I learn to take to heart what Margaret, our chief's wife and a long-time firefighter herself, tells me when I confess my sense of inadequacy. If you do one thing at a fire, she says, you've helped. Don't think of the whole fire. That's incident command's job. Most firefighting is solving one finite problem, then solving another. As the season progresses, indeed, my "one things" do start to add up, though they still seem tiny in comparison to everybody else's. By the end of that first season, I've learned to work the siren and the radio on Engine 2. I've started to learn radio protocol. I've directed traffic around a rolled truck on the freeway. I've freed hose tangled around sagebrush. A few times, I've used the hose myself at the edges of very small grass fires. Once or twice, I've even forgotten briefly that I wanted to run away.

I've also gained interesting new vocabulary words. By the end of that first summer, I've learned that "candle" can be used as a verb and that "in the black" is where firefighters like to be. I've become accustomed to hearing the nouns "structure" and "vehicle" used to mean huge classes of objects, though in my heart I doubt the usefulness of a term that includes dilapidated sheds and million-dollar houses. I can't help but remember how hard I work with my students on exact diction, and I take some comfort when it is Paul who challenges the breadth of reference. At a fire-review meeting, he complains that a property owner directed him with particular urgency to defend an outbuilding because it contained several "vehicles." "But come to find out," he says with disgust, "those weren't *vehicles*—they were just old piece-of-shit snow machines."

My view of the world changes, too. Summer holidays will never be the same. We cheer when rain begins to fall on July 2 and doesn't stop for five days. Every Friday afternoon, we watch the parade of campers and trucks and motorcycles into the national forest and cringe. "Go home!" we yell at them from our deck. "Where's your spark arrester? Do you have a shovel and a bucket to go with that firewood?" I begin to feel fierce proprietary interest in the stretch of national forest where I run every day. Though I know that my colleagues in biology are right and forests need fire periodically, I have now seen firsthand the smoking wreck of burned-over wildlands, and I hope in my heart that this place I love never, ever looks like that.

Somehow, I do not quit through that first year, or the next, though I'm still afraid of fire and still manage to avoid ever driving a truck. I continue to do little things. At the end of my third year, our department command changes. Our chief retires, taking the motherly Margaret with him, and Lorraine is among the nominations for his replacement. Kim, Peggy, and I have long ago revised our attitudes toward Lorraine. Kim and Lorraine have become closer ever since they narrowly escaped together from a fire driven by a sudden wind shift; Peggy and Lorraine have worked together in the Q.R. many times. For my part, I am simply grateful for her patience. When we say "firebabe" now, it is a term of respect and affection. The three of us and Ford join the faction working to convince her to seek the job. Along the way, we learn about the side of Lorraine that doubts and worries and listens to teasing more than we ever imagined. She is elected by a large majority, and she proves to be an excellent chief.

That's important, for our numbers are down. Our real estate agent has a heart attack, and his wife discovers that she is terminally ill. Several other firefighters decide that they are just too old, or move away, or change jobs and cannot respond. Sometimes only six or seven of us show up at a fire, and I know that the inevitable is soon to happen—the "one thing" that I am called on to do may soon become serious.

And it is—one afternoon in my fourth summer, there is no one but me to run the pump panel on Engine 2 during a big fire.

We respond to help another department; the fire is mercifully far from our house, diagonally across the valley, on the back side of a summit just outside city limits in rubbly, bone-dry sage and juniper country split by deep canyons. At the bottom, there are houses with barns and horses. The fire is a big one, wind-driven, started by something in the weekend parade of vehicles to somebody else's backyard. When the call comes, Ford is in town and heads directly to the scene; I follow my usual practice and arrive second at the station, climbing into the already warmed-up Engine 2 beside Tim, an energetic man in his thirties who joined the department shortly after we did. When we get to the fire, the tanker plane is already flying, and Ford is off with Lorraine in the densest smoke.

We are directed, with urgency, to "pick a house and defend it," and Tim heads just where I don't want to be, directly below the fire. I cannot whine to him as I would to Ford, so I whine inwardly as we roar into a long dirt driveway behind a cluster of houses, over dubious berms and into a nasty-looking cul de sac under the descending hillside. I tug down the hose, assuming that I'm to be the one to handle it, while Tim gets the pump panel going. But vile white smoke is pluming in two big pincers, the fire itself apparently just beyond the crest a hundred yards above us. Tim regards the smoke with alarm. "I'll take this up the hill," he yells. "You run the pump panel."

It's truth time. Though I am supposed to be competent to do at least this, I have never run a pump panel; in fact, I have retreated into stubborn denial that I ever *will* when the subject is discussed in meetings. But now I must. "Remind me," I say. As he does, it sounds surprisingly easy. All I have to do is watch the gauges, make sure he has enough pressure to pump (the throttle is just a knob to twist, clearly marked), make sure that the engine temperature stays around 180 (pull the tank fill lever to cool it off), and keep an eye on the engine gauges, especially making sure that we don't run out of gas. I can do that. "Oh," he tosses over his shoulder as he starts up the hill, "and don't forget that it gets really hot under this engine if we have to sit for a while. It's pretty easy to start a fire under the exhaust pipe. You probably want to pull down the little hose to defend the truck."

This is bad news. In his haste, Tim has parked the engine on a mound of loose tinder, wood chips and sawdust, where many winters of firewood have been cut. The back end of Engine 2 is buried in loose wood chips to the bumper. I'm not sure which stack of hose on top of the engine is "the little hose," or how to engage it if I did find it, and I vaguely remember that you have to dial the pressure down to do so, and that takes some of the pressure off the main hose, so you must be careful. But Tim is already far up the hill. And I'm suddenly surrounded by anxious homeowners. "Are you going to get it out?" one man asks. "Is it under control?" another stutters. A woman in her sixties, apparently in early shock, shakes my hand solemnly. "Thank you," she says.

This is hardly the time to start a new fire myself. "Can we help?" asks a young man wearing a muscle shirt, accompanied by his skinny girlfriend in flip flops. I start to tell them no, then remember the pond that we crossed and ask for buckets of water to wet the ground under the truck. I explain with what I hope is authority that I don't want to waste our water or lower the pressure on Tim's hose, even temporarily. And they surprise me, returning with a full wheelbarrow and a pink plastic sparkly sandbucket for a bailer.

After that, the day goes well. I soon learn from radio traffic that Ford and Lorraine are safe, solving one finite problem at a time in the company of many other firefighters (though Lorraine eventually gets a lecture from the main incident command for working the line rather than acting like a chief, so intense is her eagerness to fight fires). I *do* get nervous at one point when the wind shifts and trees are obviously candling beyond the benchline. I get even more nervous when Tim starts spraying the grass just beyond my line of sight, though I quickly conclude that the gesture is essentially a show for the fifty or sixty people who have wandered up there to "help." My wheelbarrow keeps getting filled, and no one laughs at me. The gauges on Engine 2 stay where they are, as well they might, for I am watching the dickens out of them. I bail with my pink bucket. I reassure the civilians. And I have a wonderful place to watch the air tanker, the size of a DC-10, sweeping so low up the draw that I worry about it catching the top of trucks. A helicopter goes by, dangling a bucket full of water that's leaking on purpose, and I laugh out loud.

The smoke dissipates. We are dismissed, and Tim comes down the hill. "Good job!" he says. I've done very little, I protest, but he's having none of that. When he sees the wheelbarrow and the puddles in the chips under the exhaust, he whistles. "Awesome idea," he says.

For some reason, this small excursion into responsibility changes everything. The next week, we have a pump panel training, and I pay attention. I learn which lever numbers go with which hoses on Engine 2. At our next fire, an owner-arson shed event, I make myself volunteer to run the panel, and I do it right. I'm amazed to find myself a little irritated when Bob and Ford periodically come around the engine to check on me. Over the next few weeks, I jump up on the engines to engage hose take-up reels, and I hook fill lines to hydrants. "Next, you'll hog the driving," says Kim, smiling.

I don't do that (indeed, I still don't drive at all), but I do find myself actually fighting fires. I handle hose on an expressway fire that spills into the sage, taking turns with Matt, who appears to have noticed me for the first time. Then I work another hose on my own when our second crew tires. A few weeks later at midnight, my worst fear comes true: an unidentifiable someone explodes a pipe bomb in the nature area pavilion in my national forest, starting a blaze whose glow we can see from the bottom of our street. Everybody works hard, and we stop the fire quickly, fifty yards downwind. After the big flames are out, Kim and I team up at the edge of the black and the green, opening the sagebrush roots, turning over smoldering piles, knocking down juniper flare-ups. I realize that we are doing an expanded version of what the BLM firefighter and I did—so long ago, it seems. We are very careful, and very thorough. When I finally get to bed at 3:30, I sleep soundly, knowing that the fire is really dead.

One full moon night that fourth September, we do not get back to bed at all. We're paged from sleep at 1 a.m. to fight a fire high on an open mountain slope, started by a cigarette thrown down from the winding road to the lookout, or a campfire, or lightning. It's very remote. Ford and I coax the tanker to the top of the paved road, then pile with our friends into the bed of someone's big four-wheel diesel truck for a ride up the dirt track. At the ultimate top of the road, we find Matt and Lorraine with the QR and a BLM party with its brush unit. The part of the fire still smoldering is farther above, inaccessible to vehicles, so Ford and I grab bladder bags and pulaskis and begin to climb. "Great, *water!*" says the BLM captain when we scramble out of the draw. Ford and I cooperate to use our water most efficiently, spreading the glowing wood to hiss and sputter. We douse several junipers that threaten to re-erupt. We go down for more water and do it all over again. "Good job," says a BLM crewmember, taking a break and watching us work.

By the time the fire is really out, dawn is just starting to light the edge of the ridge behind us, and the orange moon has moved into the center of the western sky. We decline invitations to join the others piling back into the truck and walk down together, facing that moon. The night is cool and sweet; we hold hands. Of all the times we've been in the mountains, we've never been out this late (or this early) together, never together seen quite this glow of pre-sunrise or felt quite this air. Our friends come by, waving and beeping from the pickup, then Matt and Lorraine, our other friends; the BLM truck follows. "You don't want a ride, do you?" the driver asks, more a statement than a question.

In three hours, we'll both be in class, another life. "Can I interest you in a breakfast date after we get the tanker back to the barn?" Ford asks, then pauses, smiling at my soot-blackened face. "You firebabe."

I turn and hug him, there on the mountain track, completely happy. I am, I realize, "like that" once again. I know that I'll never be a firebabe. But I can fight fires.

Fifteen

ORION
(1997)

CAMPING OPEN IN LAMOILLE CANYON in Nevada the weekend after Labor Day, I wake in the first dark hours of morning to see Orion rising low in the sky, sneaking just past the south wall's spires and cliffs, arcing above your sleeping form beside me. I was taught long ago that all constellations are always somewhere in the sky, but not until we moved to our house on Campbell Creek, where a waker can glimpse ghostly, unseasonable visits deep in the night through the big east window, did the lesson come home. In spite of Campbell Creek, though, Orion catches me off guard on this warm night—Orion, constellation of the year's end. When I was a child in Pennsylvania, Orion was my companion on nights in the car going home from family Christmas parties, or from the Acme market on Friday night, its presence accompanied by the soft, unhealthy smell of the car heater and often the metallic, rhythmic thumping of a tire chain that my father couldn't quite secure. Orion in Idaho has come to mean absolutely still 30-below nights, when, still giddy with each other after thirteen years of marriage, we dash out onto the deck for a moment to see the piercing stars. In the northern latitude of our mountain home, Orion anchors a season when every new minute of dark added to sunrise or sunset by Weather Channel calculations is a matter of remark.

This has hardly been an Orion sort of trip. With a younger friend, we're returning from a quick climbing expedition shoehorned around our teaching. After many years of talk, we've finally gotten to King Lear Peak, a complicated series of rocky blocks as remote as things get in the United States, out in the

Black Rock Desert of northwest Nevada. Thinking always about water, wearing sunhats and sunscreen, we clambered yesterday afternoon up a narrow, snaky canyon choked with wild rose and hawthorn. We bivouacked at the top of the viable stream, in a night of late summer thunder. This morning, we started before daylight, climbing a rough ridge between cliff bands before the sun got too hot. I stopped at the real scrambling and climbed back down to camp; you and our friend went on, to the rubbly ridge, over the gendarmes. After a while, it became evident that this was the wrong canyon, and the peak was a 2000-foot gorge and a day that we didn't have away. So you two found your way back down to me—sitting on a rock like a lizard. All day long, we were confident desert mountaineers, and, after our initial error, we made the decisions of quiet competence. We were off by 2:30, stopping for cold beer in Winnemucca by 5:30, and here in the canyon by dark, halfway home.

In the car, though, as we talked about how King Lear was still on the list, I heard a new note in your voice, a new longing in the blithe talk of coming back. And I knew what brought it. Lately, you've been working a little harder to make sure that you have the time to visit places, climb peaks, do things you've always wanted to do—for we're both hearing time rush by more audibly. God willing, we're not yet near the end of these days of mountain rambling, not by a long shot. You're still quite an athlete at 56, my love; walking behind you uphill, I still trip sometimes because I'm watching your triangle back, shoulders wide and hips tiny as Orion himself, steel calves flexing cleanly. And I'm still strong at 47; I only stopped at the scrambling this morning to save myself for the last of the year's masters races in our town next weekend— I can be city champion, again, if I simply finish. One of our friends says we're ageless, and swears that our energy keeps even our cats young.

But we both know that the seasons have slipped a little, without our noticing the moment that change began. In the old days, this afternoon we might have walked out and started again in the right place to climb King Lear—even though it meant working at night, even though it meant a tough drive back to catch our early Monday classes. We were crazy then, and I like things much better this way. But the ease with which we say that we were simply glad to be here is new, as is the pause I noticed in myself last winter before I pushed myself onto double black diamond ski runs, as is your consistent pleasure in being quiet at home. Our bodies have changed. Funny, that we who have lived by our brains and vitality must acknowledge at last that handsome young looks have mattered so much to us. I'm struggling to make peace with a body that can't eat and drink everything and stay thin, no matter how many miles I run a week. In the last year or so, too, that change has come to my face that came to my grandmother's at just this age—I'm suddenly middle-aged. Your beard is grey—when did that happen?—and your body and face have changed, too. When you fell hard on the ice last winter and, dazed, had to lie down, I saw the shadow of the careful years to come, though you were up and making dinner an hour later.

    Our parents are well into those careful years now, needing our attention more and more. Your mother—always exact of speech and firm of purpose—wanders increasingly in the paths of confusion; mine must daily check her cholesterol and blood pressure and has trouble walking around a block. Both of our fathers are gone. Even my ageless grandmother, still living alone in her own apartment at 98, is showing wear, shrinking to a delicate fossil of herself, skin more and more transparent even as she grumbles about not being able to wash her baseboards and bake her pies. A few years ago, in a day of exasperation filled with problems from both your son and your mother, we looked at each other and said, "We're the grownups." Then it seemed funny and made us feel important; lately, I'm remembering that "grownup" is part of a sequence.

We've always known, of course, that aging would come, was biding its time quietly below our horizon. But I realize now that I was teaching myself to deal with death when I thought about the future, not with the long in-between that we're beginning, God willing. How will we live in this new season? I've always detested the aging who cling to youth—foxy grandmas advertising with bumper stickers, George Burns leering in a more unfocused direction each day. Yet giving up is unthinkable, too. One friend your age said, "I'm too old for that" when we asked him to go hiking last year, and, suddenly, he was. I can't imagine us like that.

I know that we're among the lucky ones. Some of our friends are seriously ill; some are caught in depression or in bodies already weakening. Compared to them, what we're signing away at this point is trivial. We'll never ski the High Rustler together; I'll never again weigh 115 pounds; you'll never climb 5.10 again; attractive strangers will never again slow their cars to look at us. We're beginning these changes together and strong, with a kind of growing love we never imagined when we were young. And we have many things besides mountains to fill us: our writing, our teaching, our curiosity about the world. I have, too, the answer my faith gives—that the seeming end is a beginning—and, though you're among "the unchurched," as they say, I know that this is true for you, too.

But, for all of this, I can't help but think how much I will miss these aspen trees and limestone cliffs when no thermarest is thick enough for sleeping open. How will I live without seeing your easy, loping stride in the mountains, your turning to smile at me as I come up to you, happy in my own strength? What will we be like when "the list" is just a memory, and we can only watch Orion, high in the sky, from the window? On nights when I think of this, despite my faith, I ache. And I turn to you, as I do now, arm over your sleeping bag, head buried in your muscular back, saying, "My love, oh, my love—."

Sixteen

ORDINARY TIME
(1993)

THANKS TO MY FATHER, I am a baseball fan; thanks to the fact that I live far from any major league team, I am now a cable Braves fan. So I remember vividly how, in the fall of 1992, in the bottom of the ninth inning, in the seventh game of the divisional playoff, the Braves came back to score three runs to beat the Pirates. It was a wonderful moment—a two-out drive by a young bench player, Francisco Cabrera, with slow Sid Bream sliding across the plate milliseconds ahead of the throw to win the series. The image of the pile of Braves, the absolute crazy joy of the moment, has stayed with me for a long time.

As I watched, though, I found myself thinking about how those temporary heroes would feel the next morning, or two days on, when they woke again to their own regular lives. Francisco Cabrera might find himself getting into his car, as usual, to drive to the park for practice, turning on the radio as he always did, or Sid Bream might make coffee in the morning to the same local newscast. I imagined them feeling marooned in the regular, pinching themselves to remember.

I know, and I think everyone knows, what such moments of awakening after great excitement, great joy are like. In a sense, the "waking" is literal, for calling back the joy gets harder every morning; the moment of wonder seems more and more like it happened to someone else, and one starts needing the pictures, rereading the journal entries, holding the physical publications. As an adult, I've had my share of heightened moments: realizing that I would marry the person I loved best, winning a teaching award, giving papers in places that mattered much to me at the time, finishing my marathons. In every case, I've held on tight for a while, reluctant to fade back into my own life, sure that I'd be changed forever—yet finally awakening to that feeling of being beached, caught in an eddy, deposited weirdly in a quiet, familiar place with new echoes.

As a child, I hated those retreats to business as usual. I'd be depressed for a month when summer camp ended and school started, silently saying my camp nickname to myself when I was alone, hugging it close so I wouldn't have to be myself again. I got wrenching colitis after proms. I saved my chocolate Easter bunnies through the summer, until they became such loathsome objects in the Pennsylvania heat and humidity that even I wasn't too upset about throwing them away. But as I've grown older, I've come to cherish the onset of these business-as-usual stretches, to look ahead with happy anticipation to the quiet return of normalcy.

My church has a name for these lulls that make up the bulk of one's life: "ordinary time," it calls them. In the Catholic calendar, "ordinary time" is the term for periods that fall between the great times of preparation. The great festivals of Advent, Christmas, Lent, Easter, and Pentecost block out the year; all the leftover days, all the stretches of weeks in the down times of January and early February, summer, and fall are ordinary time. Weeks are named by sequence, as in "The Twenty-First Week In Ordinary Time"—but there's nothing special about them. The church has no unusual decorations, and one isn't obliged to be doing anything outstanding—not especially getting one's life in order, not doing penance, not celebrating, not not drinking—just living. Homilies in ordinary time tend to mention remembering the dedication of Lent, the joy of Christmas, as if priests assume that people will drift in these undemanding stretches, will need calling to attention.

As a teenager and young adult, I did indeed call myself to attention repeatedly during the times when "nothing" was happening in my life—though not in any way that any priest would encourage. I felt like I was suffocating in the mundane, like my life was doomed to a round of boredom forever. So, I contrived crises—imagining slights that plunged me into moody tears when I was a teenager, picking fights when I was married the first time, falling wildly in hopeless love. It wasn't always pleasant—but at least I knew that I was alive, that I was truly a romantic heroine and not something out of *Better Homes and Gardens*. As I think back on those years now, living always at a high-pitched crisis seems horribly exhausting, and horribly wasteful. I watch some of my students doing it, and I feel sorry for them; I watch a close friend, my age, *still* doing it, and I am amazed at her energy and her capacity for trauma, as she seems to be in the process of blowing up yet another marriage for true love. One of the problems of addiction to transcendent moments is that it's hard to get any real work done—not simply the making-a-living sort of thing, but the work that defines the self. I did very little writing when I was constantly in elation and crisis in my youth, and I taught distractedly. Even recently, when I'm in the middle of a period of great joy, I tend to be flighty; if I write at all, it's sop and cliché, no matter how good I think the work is at the time. In the business-as-usual times, in contrast, the good ideas come unbidden and often inconveniently: singing in my head while I'm doing library work in Helena, Montana on an unrelated project, so loudly at 4 a.m. that they finally wake me and drive me to use motel stationery to write an essay; giving me the connection in an academic article when I'm walking home from school after talking to freshmen all afternoon; handing me the next idea for a project when I run the lulling five-mile course I travel two or three days out of every six. When I'm doing a serious run, like a set of intervals or an 18-miler, I can only think about what I'm doing at the moment—a convenient metaphor.

Another difficult aspect of cameo moments for me is that they make me a little insane with expectations for myself—as if I'm betraying myself if the joy ever wears off, as if I'm betraying the moment if I can't keep up the pitch of accomplishment. When I was the new Distinguished Teacher of the Year, for instance, and a student dozed off in class, slumping under his Polaris hat in the back row, or when students cried in my office about grades, I felt horribly guilty. The terrible suspicion that I really didn't deserve the award kept looming; the idea reappeared from my adolescence that I was a sham and an impostor and would be revealed at any moment. For a year, I had to do everything absolutely right, or I was a failure. Now, five years on, I've cheerfully readjusted myself and can write off the occasional dozing students, the criers, the "this is *so* boring" looks. The year after the award was the most miserable of my teaching career, and it's a relief to be my old anonymous self. Constantly driving oneself to prepare the way of the Lord *perfectly* gets pretty taxing if it continues for any extended period.

In ordinary time, in contrast, surprises are free to happen—unlike the occasions when one expects wonder, and wonder doesn't come. New Year's Eve was always a let-down when I was a young adult, and the vacations I looked forward to the most were often the most dull. When I think of joyful times in my second marriage, on the other hand, I always include a day in the Ruby Mountains in Nevada—I can't remember the exact month or year, the time is so anonymous in memory. The day started out as a simple next-to-last day of a backpacking trip, when my husband and I wandered up and down ten miles, ridge after ridge, enjoying each other's company—it was one of those days when we were on the same rhythm of quiet and talk. Then we realized that we had both been thinking about walking out to "roast lamb night" at the Star in Elko, and, though the afternoon was late, we decided to push ourselves. After seven more miles and 1500 more vertical feet, we found ourselves in the middle of a grand rehearsal dinner with bride, groom, and thirty Basques in the restaurant, where we were cheerfully welcomed in. I think also of pots of bulbs that I decided on impulse to give my grandmother, for no reason, and how happy they made her; I think of nondescript Sundays when I suddenly understood a reading and found myself in tears in church; or classes I didn't plan all that well beforehand that no one wanted to leave when time was up.

It may be that I'm just getting older and lazier and less resilient, that I am indeed becoming something out of *Better Homes and Gardens*. But I don't think so. In fact, I think that the Catholic liturgy tacitly acknowledges what I've come to realize about ordinary time. For, in the high seasons of preparation, a curious thing happens to the mass: the Gloria, the song of praise for the beauty of the world, disappears. We are busy doing other things—sprinkling holy water, listening to long readings, getting our ashes—and, to make time for them, the priest passes over the Gloria's place in the sequence. In ordinary time, though, the Gloria is *always* there—we stop, take an extraordinary stretch of five or six minutes, and *celebrate*. By this pattern of exclusion and inclusion, the liturgy seems to be acknowledging that only in ordinary time, when we have space and leisure to look around, can we really appreciate what's out there. For myself, I know that it's in the simpler periods that I have the best freedom to enjoy what I have, and the energy to be grateful for it—to sing the Gloria, whether in secular or in religious terms.

This year, when the holidays were over, I was a little sad, but my *relief* surprised me. I'm glad it's January 12; I'm glad that, for now, I have no grant applications out, no manuscripts being considered, no chairmanships or athletic challenges pending. I didn't envy the Braves in that October of 1992, and I don't envy my close friend now.

I can't imagine living without the great festivals, the great peaks of life, but my childhood assurance that these were supposed to be the best parts of life has changed. The grand images may stay in one's memory, and they may be what one uses for a summary of one's life for others. But it is in ordinary time, I think now, that one *lives*.

Seventeen

SLEEPING IN THE SUN
(1999)

Wheeler and Elizabeth the cats are sixteen now, but their love of sleeping in the sun is not a consequence of age. They have always slept thus, from the time that they were kittens, in a pile or alone: Wheeler's grey head sprawled on Elizabeth's white back in a chair at midday, his lankiness stretched full length to catch the pool of light on the winter carpet; her tiny curl under the spring bird feeder, where she has forgotten what she was about and snores while finches pick at seed inches from her head. They are active cats, and they hunt successfully even in old age, but napping in the sun is arguably their favorite hobby. We have become so accustomed to their habit that we have a verb for it: suncatting. When we stumble home exhausted in late afternoon with piles of student papers still to read and find them basking, Ford has observed more than once, with a little edge, that we seem to work primarily to provide a place for cats to sleep in the sun.

Though I, too, envy them on those busy days, I like to think about what a gift we've given them, how rare it is in real life for little animals to be able to doze in broad daylight as thoughtlessly as ours do. The tiny animals I see when I hike are always moving, always just going out of sight; if they sleep, it's in dark places, hiding against all the things that want to do them harm. I've seen big cats sleeping in the sun in zoos: tigers yawning on boulders at first warm fall light, lions sprawled in piles echoing Wheeler and Elizabeth. But in the wild they, too, must often have to take turns, knowing that other big cats, humans, or something else may be watching them. Oblivion in public is a rare luxury in their world, and a dangerous one.

For Wheeler and Elizabeth, though, days are safe times, the odd eagle hunting the deck or rogue neighborhood dog aside. They are free to sprawl boneless, so warm sometimes that I fear that their fur will begin to smoke. They are free to be careless, and lucky beyond their ability to know.

We are driving through the Columbia Gorge this rainy April afternoon, remarking on the spring face of this place we know so well, drifts of daffodils on the freeway banks at Hood River, flush of celadon lighting the oaks that we never notice at other seasons among the dark pines. We've never been here in April before, and shouldn't be now—we should be in Tuscany. We've planned that trip for a year and a half, working all summer and extra in fall to earn this spring as flex time, parsing Italian to our tapes daily, collecting stacks of guidebooks that avalanche next to the bed when we rise in the night. This is a consolation prize trip. It's also a first attempt to clear our minds by changing our place as we wait for the first phase of Ford's treatment to work so that we can go on to the scarier, longer phases ahead.

Just before we were to leave for Italy, we learned that Ford had cancer, treatable but serious. "We think a good prognosis, *but . . .*" have become words that we're already tired of hearing from the doctors. In the first week or two, I was sure that someone had made a stupid, actionable mistake, filing the wrong records with the wrong name. Ford couldn't be sick. But he has been to three doctors now, and each has examined him, and we must acknowledge that he is. We've just spent three weeks reading everything we can find on prostate cancer—articles friends send from medical journals, internet postings by the informed and the dangerous. And books that make me dizzy when I even take them off the shelf in the public library, much less open them, books that I've considered smuggling past the magnetic gate, so blindingly, irrationally horrified am I that a librarian will see. It's not shame, so much as knowing that if any sympathy is offered I will lose control, something I do even in the house when Ford isn't there, weeping as I sit in the big chair by the window watching magpies play on the neighbors' barn roof below.

We're lucky to have this semester off, we tell each other, and it's true—time to consider our choices, to talk to doctors, to simply *be* with the news. Now, after three weeks, we have made a plan, and begun it, and we must wait for the rest. So, this trip—the Gorge in a new time of year, a diversion and a comfort, we hope.

It's only partly working. Like my own house, like the magpies, the Gorge looks fake to me, too indifferently picturesque, too much itself when everything has changed. Ford is doing so much better than I am, cheerful, remarking on the odd spring softness of the rain, the different drift of mist this time of year. I wish that I could see that.

Then a song begins to play on the car radio, a cheaply uplifting A.M. hit from fifteen years ago by a male band with bigger hair than I have ever worn. It's homogenized and slick, and Ford reaches to change the channel. "Don't; I used to like this song," I say, and suddenly I have to turn and look out my window, tears flooding in. Suddenly, I am back, driving to Twin Falls to teach my night class in the months before we finally became *us*, in one of the darkest times, when we had been together and parted, and it looked like we were never going to find each other again, despite the baffling surety in my bones. Those damp late winter nights so long ago, I drove 112 miles each way from home for those twenty-two students, and they appreciated it, so we always finished late. In consequence, I needed something to keep me awake driving home to the apartment where I lived alone, nobody waiting up, and the only stations that the university's K-car radio could find were the most powerful rock or cowboy stations. Songs in incredibly bad taste became my anthems, the kind of songs designed as anthems for young men driving home from bars in pickup trucks who believed that they had just been foiled again in their quest for true love, and for the angry or flattened young women who had played a part in those same dances but told stories of their own. I had a lot of those songs that year, as winter began easing into a spring that I couldn't guess held redemption. "Don't stop believin'!" I sang aloud at the top of my lungs to the stars overhead, and "Don't stop thinkin' about tomorrow!"—and other lines that I am even more reluctant to recall.

How did I live through that, I wonder, no longer seeing the Gorge but the rolling highway of those nights. I feel again the constant rush of those times, the constant edginess, killing but alive, alive, nothing ever taken for granted, every day a surprise, exhausting, real. I look at Ford, who has changed the station to find the sort of country anthems that *he* favors, and I remember how he used to look, before we became so blissfully comfortable together. Ford the other—that's something I haven't seen for a long time. I remember seeing him that way in the first years of our marriage, when, for all our promises, we could have come apart at any time. I can't remember when things changed. The growing together was so gradual, the steps into comfort with each other so small, that it seems like we've always had this luxurious understanding.

We've been sleeping in the sun together for a long time now. I know what he's thinking almost all the time, though I don't always like it, and he knows my thoughts. We're sure of our love—not in a taking-for-granted way, for no one who came together as late as we did could lapse that far, but calmly, happily. We have been the ground against which the world stood. When we have worried, it has mostly been about little spot fires of problems—

ugly for a moment, but easy to contain. For fourteen years, we've never doubted that tomorrow would soon be here, and that it would be good.

I know that most people don't ever have this, any more than most little animals do. Through most of time, humans have had to be a species with one eye open, watching for the predator, the human enemy, the random chance that could blow the day apart. The two of us and our cohort are almost alone in history. War has been distant, not just over the next ridge; hunger is something we have never faced. In Idaho, we can still leave doors unlocked; not farmers, we can watch the Weather Channel for fun. I think of my father, aware every moment of the money he had to pile between us and the fears of his own childhood. I think of all the married people we know who have felt that ache begin: he's become an other I don't know; she's gone, though she's still across the table—how long will it be until she leaves? I think of our students with cars that don't start on exam days, and of the people who will never be our students. We're not rich, and we don't have perfect jobs, and we've thought that our troubles were many at times. But when we've touched the way that most humans live, we've always noticed the difference. When I spent a summer in Washington, D.C., the necessary constant watchfulness every step from my apartment exhausted me; when we fight fires that turn trailer houses into stinking shells, we wonder together afterward in the kitchen what the people will do, and the wondering keeps us awake.

We're going to be more like them from now on, I realize, never again able to ignore what might be waiting just over the ridge, beyond the firelight. I feel the rush of adrenaline, the ache so common in the past few weeks, and I recognize it now as a constant companion from fifteen years ago. Join the human race, I think; who knows what you'll be able to see with your eyes open? But I am out of practice now, and I am angry and afraid. What will we do? I wonder. How will we stand this?

Six months later, we fly back from Ford's surgery in Seattle. As far as we know, things have gone well. During radiation treatments at home we walked our five or six miles together almost every day, though slower, with more noticing. Ford is hale and funny and apparently strong three days after the operation delivering internal radiation. We threw away the appalling, unnecessary, side effects treatment pack before we left Seattle. We're going home together, despite my fears that Ford would die in this relatively easy, outpatient procedure, and we're still ourselves.

We pass Rainier, almost touching distance, boilerplate glaciers gleaming; we talk skiing for the winter ahead. We drink the free glasses of wine that this airline serendipitously dispenses. I'm *happy*, I realize to my surprise, blindingly happy, taking this ordinary airplane ride, coming home to our house. We won't know the efficacy of this treatment for a year, and yet, somehow, that doesn't matter now. Today is enough, this amazing time together, simply looking at Ford and at the mountain over his shoulder, holding his hand. And, when we're home, greeted by Elizabeth and Wheeler stretching as if they'd slept for this whole week we've been away, and we sit on the deck and watch the light fade, it still doesn't matter.

I know that this is what's supposed to happen, the absolutely tritest insight, but I don't care. I love *seeing* Ford; I love thinking about our life together as a gift. I'm even getting a little bit used to the daily realization that I must find a reason to believe today, and that today is what we have.

This is not, however, a perfect parable about a fortunate fall. I do often find myself "wasting regretful thought," as Hawthorne would say, on the years that we were allowed to sleep in the sun; I wish that we were sprawled there still. I'm often angry, and I'm often afraid. But I'm just as often surprised at how lucky I still feel

Sleeping in the Sun 119

now that I'm keeping one eye open, how sweet the pleasures of a single day can be.

One morning I wake from a dream—a dream about that long-ago spring in which we do *not* find each other again—to find Ford smiling at me. *We'll live*, I think, as consciousness returns, borrowing his long-time remark after crisis or excess, and I'm amazed at myself and at this moment.

We'll live.

About the Author

Susan Swetnam was born in the northern suburbs of Philadelphia and earned her B.A. and M.A. from the University of Delaware and her Ph.D. from the University of Michigan, where she was a Rackham Scholar and specialized in narrative theory and the history of the novel. Before interviewing for a job at Idaho State University (ISU) in 1979, she had never been west of Kalamazoo, Michigan, but from the moment the plane landed, she knew she had found the place where she was supposed to be.

Susan has taught English at ISU for more than twenty years, earning the University's Distinguished Teacher, Distinguished Public Servant, and Outstanding Researcher awards. She served as Chair of the Idaho Humanities Council in the late 1980s and has been very active in the Council's work around the state for many years. Her first book, a study of narrative patterns in Mormon pioneer autobiography and biography, entitled *Lives of the Saints in Southeast Idaho: An Introduction to Mormon Pioneer Life Story Writing*, was published by the University of Idaho Press in 1990. She has written essays and articles that have appeared in national and regional magazines, including *Gourmet*, *Walking*, *Mademoiselle*, *Handwoven*, *Journal of the West*, and *Rendezvous*. A number of her writings have been anthologized in various collections, including *Where the Morning Light's Still Blue: Personal Essays About Idaho* (University of Idaho Press, 1994).

Susan's physical recreation includes running, competitive racewalking, skiing, and mountaineering. Other interests include knitting, gardening, and cooking. She is a member of the St. Joseph's Parish Council in Pocatello and leads a Girl Scout troop. Susan is married to poet and teacher Ford Swetnam.